JAVASCRIPT
PROGRAMMING FOR
ABSOLUTE BEGINNERS

Mastering the Basics of JavaScript Coding for Web Development and Beyond

RICHARD D. CROWLEY

Table of Contents

Introduction

Welcome to the World of JavaScript

Absolutely. Let's dive deep into the introduction of "JavaScript Programming for Absolute Beginners," expanding on the core concepts of "Why JavaScript?" and "The Role of JavaScript in Web Development and Beyond" to create a compelling and educational foundation.

Introduction: Welcome to the World of JavaScript

JavaScript, a language that began its journey as a simple scripting tool for web browsers, has evolved into a powerhouse that drives the interactive web and extends far beyond.[1] It's the language that brings dynamism to static web pages, powers complex web applications, and even ventures into server-side development, mobile apps, and beyond.[2] This introduction aims to demystify JavaScript, emphasizing its power, versatility, and the crucial role it plays in the modern digital landscape.[3]

1.1. Why JavaScript? Understanding Its Power and Versatility

- **The Ubiquity of the Web:**
  - JavaScript's primary domain is the web.[4] Every modern web browser supports JavaScript, making it the de facto language for front-end web development.[5] This ubiquity means that once you learn JavaScript, you can reach a vast audience across countless devices.[6]
  - Unlike other languages that might require specific environments or plugins, JavaScript runs directly in the

browser, ensuring a consistent user experience.[7]

- **Interactivity and Dynamic Content:**
    - Before JavaScript, web pages were largely static.[8] JavaScript allowed developers to manipulate the Document Object Model (DOM), enabling the creation of dynamic content that responds to user actions.[9]
    - Examples abound: interactive forms, dynamic image galleries, real-time updates, and engaging animations.[10] JavaScript makes these experiences possible.
- **Client-Side Processing:**
    - JavaScript executes on the client-side (the user's browser), which reduces the load on servers.[11] This client-side processing results in faster response times and a more fluid user experience.[12]

- For instance, form validation can be performed instantly in the browser, without requiring a round trip to the server.[13]
- **A Language of Evolution:**
  - JavaScript has undergone significant evolution, especially with the introduction of ECMAScript 6 (ES6) and subsequent versions.[14] These updates have introduced new features and syntax that make JavaScript more powerful and expressive.[15]
  - Features like arrow functions, classes, modules, and promises have transformed JavaScript into a modern and sophisticated language.[16]
- **Versatility Beyond the Browser:**
  - While JavaScript's roots are in the browser, its versatility extends far beyond.[17] With Node.js, JavaScript can be used

for server-side development, building scalable and efficient web applications.[18]

- Frameworks like React Native and Ionic enable developers to use JavaScript to build cross-platform mobile applications.[19]
- Javascript is also used in IOT(Internet of Things) devices, and desktop applications.[20]

- **A Thriving Ecosystem:**
  - JavaScript boasts a vast and active community, contributing to a rich ecosystem of libraries, frameworks, and tools.[21]
  - This ecosystem provides developers with a wealth of resources, making it easier to build complex applications and solve challenging problems.[22]

1.2. The Role of JavaScript in Web Development and Beyond

- **Front-End Web Development:**
  - JavaScript is the cornerstone of front-end web development.[23] It's used to create interactive user interfaces, handle user input, and manipulate the DOM.[24]
  - Frameworks like React, Vue, and Angular leverage JavaScript to build complex single-page applications (SPAs) that deliver rich and engaging user experiences.[25]
- **Back-End Web Development:**
  - Node.js has revolutionized back-end development by allowing developers to use JavaScript on the server-side.[26]
  - This enables full-stack JavaScript development, where

developers can use a single language for both the front-end and back-end.[27]

- Node.js is used to build API's, and servers that handle large amounts of traffic.[28]

- **Mobile App Development:**
  - React Native and Ionic have made JavaScript a viable option for mobile app development.[29]
  - These frameworks allow developers to build cross-platform mobile apps that can run on both iOS and Android, reducing development time and costs.[30]

- **Desktop Application Development:**
  - Electron.js allows for the creation of cross platform desktop applications.[31] Applications like Discord, and Slack, are created with electron.[32]

- **Game Development:**
  - JavaScript is increasingly used in game development, especially for browser-based games.[33]
  - Libraries like Phaser and PixiJS provide tools for creating 2D and 3D games using JavaScript.
- **Internet of Things (IoT):**
  - JavaScript is finding its way into IoT devices, enabling developers to create smart and connected devices.[34]
  - Node.js and other JavaScript-based platforms are used to build IoT applications that can interact with sensors and actuators.[35]
- **Expanding Horizons:**
  - JavaScript's versatility and adaptability continue to drive its expansion into new domains.[36]
  - Machine learning, data visualization, and even robotics

are areas where JavaScript is making significant strides.[37]

- ○ Cloud computing platforms are also using javascript more and more.[38]

Educational Importance:

For absolute beginners, understanding these foundational aspects is crucial. It sets the stage for a deeper dive into the language, providing context and motivation. By grasping why JavaScript is so powerful and versatile, learners can appreciate the significance of their journey and the potential that lies ahead.

This detailed exploration of the introduction provides a robust foundation, setting the stage for the reader to understand the power and usefulness of javascript.

1.3. Setting Up Your Development Environment: Tools and Resources

Before you can start writing JavaScript, you need a suitable environment. This section will guide you through the essential tools and resources, ensuring you have a smooth and productive learning experience.

- **The Text Editor: Your Coding Canvas**
  - A text editor is where you'll write and edit your JavaScript code. While simple text editors like Notepad or TextEdit can work, dedicated code editors offer features that significantly enhance your workflow.
  - **Recommended Options:**
    - **Visual Studio Code (VS Code):** A free, open-source editor from

Microsoft, VS Code is highly popular for its versatility, extensive extensions, and built-in debugging tools.[1] It supports JavaScript and many other languages.[2]

- **Sublime Text:** A fast and powerful text editor with a clean interface and excellent performance.[3]

- **Atom:** Another free, open-source editor with a customizable interface and a wide range of packages.[4]

- **Choosing the Right Editor:** Consider factors like ease of use, features, and community support. VS Code is generally recommended for beginners due to its user-friendly interface and robust features.[5]

- **The Web Browser: Your Execution Platform**
  - Since JavaScript is primarily a client-side language, you'll need a web browser to run your code.[6] All modern browsers have built-in JavaScript engines and developer tools.[7]
  - **Recommended Browsers:**
    - **Google Chrome:** Chrome's developer tools are highly regarded for their comprehensive debugging capabilities.[8]
    - **Mozilla Firefox:** Firefox also offers excellent developer tools and is known for its privacy-focused approach.[9]
    - **Edge:** The newest version of Microsoft edge is also a very capable browser.
  - **Developer Tools:**

- Browsers' developer tools are indispensable for debugging, inspecting elements, and monitoring network activity.[10]
- Key features include:
    - **Console:** Used to display log messages, execute JavaScript code, and view errors.
    - **Elements:** Allows you to inspect and modify the HTML and CSS of a web page.[11]
    - **Sources/Debugger:** Used to set breakpoints, step through code, and inspect variables.
    - **Network:** Monitors network requests and responses.[12]

- **Node.js: Expanding Beyond the Browser**
  - Node.js is a runtime environment that allows you to execute JavaScript code outside of a web browser.[13]
  - It's essential for server-side JavaScript development and using command-line tools.
  - **Installation:** Download and install Node.js from the official website (nodejs.org).[14] Node.js comes with npm (Node Package Manager), which is used to install and manage JavaScript libraries.[15]
- **Online Code Editors: Quick and Convenient**
  - For quick experimentation and learning, online code editors provide a convenient way to write and run JavaScript code without installing any software.[16]
  - **Popular Options:**

- **CodePen:** A social development environment for front-end web developers.[17]
- **JSFiddle:** A simple and easy-to-use online code editor.[18]
- **Repl.it:** A versatile online IDE that supports multiple languages, including JavaScript.[19]

- **Resources for Learning:**
  - **Mozilla Developer Network (MDN):** MDN is an invaluable resource for JavaScript documentation, tutorials, and examples.[20]
  - **W3Schools:** Provides comprehensive tutorials and examples for web development technologies, including JavaScript.
  - **YouTube:** Many excellent YouTube channels offer

JavaScript tutorials and courses.[21]

- ○ **Online Courses:** Platforms like Coursera, Udemy, and freeCodeCamp offer structured JavaScript courses.[22]
- ○ **Books:** "Eloquent JavaScript" and "You Don't Know JS" are highly recommended books for JavaScript learners.[23]

1.4. Your First Steps: "Hello, World!" and Basic Syntax Overview

Now that you have your development environment set up, it's time to write your first JavaScript code.

- **"Hello, World!" in the Browser:**
  - ○ **Creating an HTML File:**

- Create a new file named index.html and add the following code:

HTML

```
<!DOCTYPE html>
<html>
<head>
 <title>Hello, World!</title>
</head>
<body>
 <script>
  console.log("Hello, World!");
 </script>
</body>
</html>
```

* **Opening in the Browser:**
  * Open the `index.html` file in your web browser.

* **Viewing the Console:**
    * Open the browser's developer tools (usually by pressing F12 or right-clicking and selecting "Inspect").
    * Go to the "Console" tab.
    * You should see the message "Hello, World!" displayed in the console.
* **Explanation:**
    * The `<script>` tag is used to embed JavaScript code within an HTML document.
    * `console.log()` is a function that displays a message in the browser's console.

* **"Hello, World!" in Node.js:**
    * **Creating a JavaScript File:**
        * Create a new file named hello.js and add the following code:

JavaScript

```
console.log("Hello, World!");
```

* **Running the Code:**
    * Open your terminal or command prompt.
    * Navigate to the directory where you saved the `hello.js` file.
    * Run the command `node hello.js`.
    * You should see the message "Hello, World!" displayed in the terminal.

- **Basic Syntax Overview:**
    - **Variables:** Used to store data.
        - `let message = "Hello, JavaScript!";`
    - **Data Types:**
        - Strings: "Hello"
        - Numbers: 42
        - Booleans: true or false
    - **Operators:** Used to perform operations.

- Arithmetic: +, -, *, /
- Comparison: ==, ===, !=, !==, >, <
- Logical: && (and), || (or), ! (not)
  - **Conditional Statements:** Used to make decisions.
    - if (condition) { // code } else { // code }
  - **Loops:** Used to repeat actions.
    - for (let i = 0; i < 10; i++) { // code }
    - while (condition) { // code }
  - **Functions:** Used to create reusable code blocks.
    - function greet(name) { console.log("Hello, " + name + "!"); }
- **Comments:**
  - Single-line comments: // This is a comment
  - Multi-line comments: /* This is a multi-line comment */

By completing these initial steps, you've taken your first steps into the world of JavaScript. Remember that practice and exploration are key to mastering any programming language.

CHAPTER 1

Foundations of JavaScript: Variables and Data Types

Variables and data types are fundamental to any programming language, and JavaScript is no exception.[1] They allow us to store, manipulate, and represent data within our programs, enabling us to build complex and dynamic applications.

1.1. Declaring and Initializing Variables: var, let, and const

Variables are like containers that hold data.[2] In JavaScript, we declare variables using the keywords var, let, and const. Each keyword has its own characteristics and use cases.

- var **(Function-Scoped):**[3]
  - var was the original way to declare variables in JavaScript.

- Variables declared with var are function-scoped, meaning they are accessible within the function in which they are declared, or globally if declared outside any function.
- var variables are hoisted, which means their declarations are moved to the top of their scope during compilation, though their initializations remain in place. This can lead to unexpected behavior if not handled carefully.
- Example:

•

JavaScript

```
function exampleVar() {
  if (true) {
    var x = 10;
  }
```

```
    console.log(x); // Output: 10 (x is
accessible here)
}
exampleVar();

function exampleVarHoisting() {
    console.log(y); //output: undefined.
    var y = 5;
}
exampleVarHoisting();
```

- let **(Block-Scoped):**[6]
    - let was introduced in ECMAScript 6 (ES6) to address the limitations of var.
    - Variables declared with let are block-scoped, meaning they are accessible only within the block (e.g., within an if statement, for loop, or function) in which they are declared.
    - let variables are also hoisted, but they are not initialized until

their declaration is evaluated. Accessing a let variable before its declaration results in a ReferenceError.

o Example:

●

JavaScript

```
function exampleLet() {
 if (true) {
  let x = 10;
  console.log(x); // Output: 10
 }
 //console.log(x); // Error: x is not defined
(x is not accessible here)
}
exampleLet();
```

● const **(Block-Scoped, Constant):**[7]

o const is also block-scoped and was introduced in ES6.

- const is used to declare constants, which are variables whose values cannot be reassigned after initialization.
- Like let, const variables are hoisted but not initialized until their declaration is evaluated.
- const variables must be initialized when they are declared.
- It is important to note that when const is used with objects or arrays, the contents of the object or array can be changed, but the variable can not be reassigned.
- Example:

●

JavaScript

```
function exampleConst() {
  const PI = 3.14159;
  console.log(PI); // Output: 3.14159
```

```
  //PI = 3.14; // Error: Assignment to
constant variable.
}
exampleConst();

function exampleConstArray(){
  const myArray =;
  myArray.push(4);
  console.log(myArray); //output:
  //myArray =; //error.
}
exampleConstArray();
```

- **Best Practices:**
    - Use const by default for variables whose values will not change.
    - Use let for variables whose values may change.
    - Avoid using var in modern JavaScript code.

1.2. Understanding Data Types: Numbers, Strings, Booleans, and More

Data types define the kind of data that a variable can hold. JavaScript is a dynamically typed language, which means that the type of a variable is determined at runtime, and a variable can hold values of different types throughout its lifetime.[8]

- **Numbers:**
  - Numbers represent numeric values.[9] JavaScript has a single number type that can represent both integers and floating-point numbers.[10]
  - Example:

JavaScript

```
let integer = 42;
let floatingPoint = 3.14;
```

```
let negative = -10;
```

- **Strings:**
  - Strings represent sequences of characters.[11] They are used to store text.
  - Strings can be enclosed in single quotes ('...'), double quotes ("..."), or backticks (\...``).
  - Backticks allow for string interpolation, which enables you to embed variables within strings.[12]
  - Example:

JavaScript

```
let singleQuoted = 'Hello, World!';
let doubleQuoted = "JavaScript is awesome!";
```

```
let templateLiteral = `The answer is
${integer}.`; //string interpolation
```

- **Booleans:**
    - Booleans represent logical values: true or false.
    - Booleans are used in conditional statements and logical operations.[13]
    - Example:

JavaScript

```
let isTrue = true;
let isFalse = false;
```

- null **and** undefined**:**
    - null represents the intentional absence of a value. It is often

used to indicate that a variable or object has no value.
- undefined represents a variable that has been declared but not assigned a value.
- Example:

JavaScript

```
let nothing = null;
let unknown; // undefined
```

- **Objects:**
  - Objects are complex data types that represent collections of key-value pairs.[14]
  - Objects are used to represent real-world entities and data structures.[15]
  - Example:

JavaScript

```
let person = {
  name: "John Doe",
  age: 30,
  city: "New York"
};
```

- **Arrays:**
  - ○ Arrays are ordered collections of values.
  - ○ Arrays can hold values of any data type.[16]
  - ○ Example:

JavaScript

```
let numbers = ;
let mixed = ;
```

- **Symbols:**
  - Symbols are unique and immutable values that are used as object property keys.[17]
  - Symbols were introduced in ES6.[18]
  - Example:

JavaScript

```
let uniqueId = Symbol("id");
```

- **BigInt:**
  - BigInt is a numeric data type that can represent integers of arbitrary precision.[19]
  - BigInts were introduced in ES2020.
  - Example:

JavaScript

```
let bigIntValue = 9007199254740991n;
```

Understanding variables and data types is essential for building robust and reliable JavaScript applications. By mastering these foundational concepts, you can effectively store, manipulate, and represent data within your programs.

1.3. Working with Operators: Arithmetic, Comparison, and Logical

Operators are symbols that perform operations on values and variables.[1] JavaScript provides a rich set of operators, enabling you to perform arithmetic calculations, compare values, and combine logical conditions.

- **Arithmetic Operators:**

- These operators perform mathematical calculations.[2]
- **Addition (+):** Adds two operands.[3]
  - let sum = 5 + 3; // sum is 8
-
- **Subtraction (-):** Subtracts the second operand from the first.[4]
  - let difference = 10 - 4; // difference is 6
-
- **Multiplication (*):** Multiplies two operands.
  - let product = 6 * 7; // product is 42
- **Division (/):** Divides the first operand by the second.
  - let quotient = 20 / 5; // quotient is 4
- **Modulus (%):** Returns the remainder of a division.[5]
  - let remainder = 17 % 3; // remainder is 2

- ○
  - ○ **Increment (++):** Increases the value of a variable by 1.[6]
    - let count = 0; count++; // count is 1
  - ○
  - ○ **Decrement (--):** Decreases the value of a variable by 1.[7]
    - let counter = 5; counter--; // counter is 4
  - ○
  - ○ **Exponentiation ():**** Raises the first operand to the power of the second.[8]
    - let power = 2 ** 3; // power is 8
  - ○
- **Comparison Operators:**
  - ○ These operators compare two operands and return a boolean value (true or false).
  - ○ **Equal to (==):** Checks if two operands are equal (performs type coercion).[9]

- 5 == "5"; // true (type coercion)
  -

- **Strict equal to (===)**: Checks if two operands are equal and of the same type (no type coercion).[10]
  - 5 === "5"; // false (different types)
  -

- **Not equal to (!=)**: Checks if two operands are not equal (performs type coercion).[11]
  - 10 != "10"; // false (type coercion)
  -

- **Strict not equal to (!==)**: Checks if two operands are not equal or not of the same type (no type coercion).[12]
  - 10 !== "10"; // true (different types)
  -

- o **Greater than (>):** Checks if the first operand is greater than the second.[13]
    - 15 > 12; // true
- o
- o **Less than (<):** Checks if the first operand is less than the second.[14]
    - 8 < 10; // true
- o
- o **Greater than or equal to (>=):** Checks if the first operand is greater than or equal to the second.[15]
    - 20 >= 20; // true
- o
- o **Less than or equal to (<=):** Checks if the first operand is less than or equal to the second.[16]
    - 5 <= 7; // true
- o

- **Logical Operators:**

- These operators combine boolean values and return a boolean result.[17]
- **Logical AND (&&):** Returns true if both operands are true.
  - true && true; // true
  - true && false; // false
- **Logical OR (||):** Returns true if at least one operand is true.
  - true || false; // true
  - false || false; // false
- **Logical NOT (!):** Inverts the boolean value of an operand.[18]
  - !true; // false
  - !false; // true
-

- **Assignment Operators:**
  - These operators assign values to variables.
  - =, +=, -=, *=, /=, %=
  - let x = 10; x += 5; // x is now 15

1.4. Type Conversion and Data Manipulation

JavaScript is a dynamically typed language, which means that the type of a variable can change during runtime.[19] This flexibility also requires careful management of type conversion and data manipulation.

- **Type Conversion (Type Coercion):**
  - JavaScript automatically converts data types in certain situations, known as type coercion.[20]
  - This can lead to unexpected results if not understood.
  - **Implicit Conversion:**
    - Occurs automatically when operators are used with operands of different types.[21]
    - "5" + 3; // "53" (number 3 is converted to string "3")

- "5" * 2; // 10 (string "5" is converted to number 5)
- "5" - "2" // 3 (both strings are converted to numbers)
- **Explicit Conversion:**
  - Performed using built-in functions to convert data types explicitly.[22]
- **Number():** Converts a value to a number.[23]
  - Number("123"); // 123
  - Number("abc"); // NaN (Not a Number)
-
- **String():** Converts a value to a string.[24]
  - String(123); // "123"
  - String(true); // "true"
-
- **Boolean():** Converts a value to a boolean.[25]
  - Boolean(0); // false
  - Boolean("hello"); // true
  - Boolean(""); // false

- o
- o parseInt() **and** parseFloat()**:** Parses a string and returns an integer or floating-point number.[26]
  - parseInt("10.5"); // 10
  - parseFloat("10.5"); // 10.5
- o

- **Data Manipulation:**
  - **String Manipulation:**
    - JavaScript provides various methods for manipulating strings.[27]
    - let text = "Hello, World!";
    - text.length; // 13
    - text.toUpperCase(); // "HELLO, WORLD!"
    - text.slice(0, 5); // "Hello"
    - text.replace("World", "JavaScript"); // "Hello, JavaScript!"
  - **Array Manipulation:**
    - Arrays offer many methods for adding,

removing, and modifying elements.[28]

- let numbers = ;
- numbers.push(4); // ;
- numbers.pop(); // removes the last element
- numbers.shift(); // removes the first element
- numbers.unshift(0); // adds element to the beginning
- numbers.splice(1, 2); // removes elements from index 1
- numbers.concat(); // merges arrays

- **Object Manipulation:**
  - Objects are dynamic, and their properties can be added, modified, or deleted.[29]
  - let person = { name: "John", age: 30 };
  - person.city = "New York";

- delete person.age;

Understanding operators and type conversion is crucial for writing effective JavaScript code. These tools enable you to perform calculations, make comparisons, and manipulate data, allowing you to build dynamic and interactive applications.[30]

CHAPTER 2

Controlling the Flow: Conditional Statements and Loops

The ability to dictate the order in which code executes is crucial for creating intelligent and adaptable programs. Conditional statements and loops are the tools that enable this control, allowing for decision-making and repetitive execution.

2.1. Making Decisions: if, else if, and else Statements (In-Depth)

- **The Power of Conditional Logic:**
  - Conditional statements allow programs to respond dynamically to different inputs and conditions. This is essential for creating interactive applications, handling user

input, and implementing complex logic.

- o Consider a simple scenario: a login system. Based on whether the user enters the correct credentials, the program needs to execute different actions. This is where if, else if, and else statements come into play.

- **Understanding the Flow:**
  - o The if statement evaluates a condition, and if it's true, the code within its block is executed. If the condition is false, the program moves to the next else if (if present) or else block.
  - o The else if statements are evaluated sequentially. If one of them is true, its corresponding block is executed, and the rest are skipped.
  - o The else statement acts as a catch-all, executing its block if

none of the preceding conditions are true.

- **Practical Applications:**
  - **Input Validation:**
    - Conditional statements are used to validate user input, ensuring it meets specific criteria. For example, checking if an email address is in a valid format or if a password meets minimum length requirements.
  - **Game Development:**
    - In games, conditional statements are used to handle player actions, check for collisions, and determine game outcomes. For instance, checking if a player's health is zero to determine if the game is over.
  - **Web Development:**

- Web applications use conditional statements to display different content based on user roles, preferences, or device types. For example, showing a mobile-friendly layout for users on smartphones.
- **Best Practices:**
  - **Clarity and Readability:**
    - Write clear and concise conditions that are easy to understand. Avoid overly complex nested if statements, which can make code difficult to maintain.
  - **Handling Edge Cases:**
    - Consider all possible scenarios and handle edge cases appropriately. Ensure your code behaves

predictably in all situations.

- ○ **Using Boolean Expressions:**
  - ■ Leverage boolean expressions (expressions that evaluate to true or false) to create effective conditional logic.

2.2. Repeating Actions: for, while, and do...while Loops (Expanded)

- **The Necessity of Repetition:**
  - ○ Loops are essential for automating repetitive tasks, processing large datasets, and creating dynamic animations. Without loops, you would have to write the same code multiple

times, which is inefficient and
error-prone.

- **Choosing the Right Loop:**
  - for **Loop:**
    - Use for loops when you
      know in advance how
      many times you need to
      repeat a block of code.
      This is common when
      iterating over arrays or
      performing a specific
      number of iterations.
  - while **Loop:**
    - Use while loops when you
      need to repeat a block of
      code as long as a certain
      condition is true. This is
      useful when you don't
      know in advance how
      many iterations are
      needed.
  - do...while **Loop:**
    - Use do...while loops when
      you need to ensure that a

block of code is executed at least once, regardless of the initial condition.

- **Loop Control:**
  - break **Statement:**
    - The break statement terminates the loop immediately, regardless of whether the loop condition is still true. This is useful for exiting a loop early when a specific condition is met.
  - continue **Statement:**
    - The continue statement skips the current iteration of the loop and proceeds to the next iteration. This is useful for skipping specific iterations based on certain conditions.
- **Practical Applications:**
  - **Data Processing:**

- Loops are used to process large datasets, such as arrays or files. For example, iterating over an array to calculate the sum of its elements.
  - **Animation:**
    - Loops are used to create animations by repeatedly updating the position or appearance of objects on the screen.
  - **User Interaction:**
    - Loops can be used to repeatedly prompt the user for input until a valid response is received.
- **Best Practices:**
  - **Avoiding Infinite Loops:**
    - Ensure that your loop conditions will eventually become false to prevent infinite loops, which can

cause your program to
freeze.

- **Loop Efficiency:**
  - Optimize your loops for
    performance, especially
    when dealing with large
    datasets. Avoid
    unnecessary calculations
    or operations within the
    loop.
- **Clear Loop Conditions:**
  - Write clear and concise
    loop conditions that are
    easy to understand.

By understanding and applying these
concepts, you can create programs that are
both powerful and efficient.

2.3. Using break and continue for Loop Control

- Fine-Tuning Loop Behavior:
    - While loops provide the framework for repetition, break and continue offer granular control over their execution. They allow you to modify the natural flow of a loop, enabling more sophisticated and efficient algorithms.
- break **Statement: Immediate Loop Termination:**
    - The break statement is used to terminate a loop prematurely. When encountered, it immediately exits the innermost loop, transferring control to the statement following the loop.[1]
    - Use Cases:
        - **Finding a Specific Element:** When searching for a particular element in a list or array,

you can use break to exit the loop as soon as the element is found, avoiding unnecessary iterations.

- **Error Handling:** In situations where an error condition is detected within a loop, break can be used to terminate the loop and prevent further execution.

- **Menu-Driven Programs:** In menu-driven programs, break can be used to exit the main loop when the user selects an "exit" option.

- continue **Statement: Skipping Iterations:**
  - The continue statement skips the remaining code within the current iteration of a loop and proceeds to the next iteration. It

does not terminate the loop entirely; it simply skips the current cycle.[2]

- o Use Cases:
  - ■ **Filtering Data:** When processing a list of data, continue can be used to skip elements that don't meet certain criteria.
  - ■ **Avoiding Unnecessary Calculations:** If a particular iteration of a loop is known to be irrelevant or unnecessary, continue can be used to skip it and improve performance.
  - ■ **Handling Exceptions:** When you want to handle a specific issue in a loop, but want the loop to continue its normal process, then the continue statement is very useful.

- Clarity and Readability:
  - While break and continue can be powerful tools, it's essential to use them judiciously. Overuse can make code difficult to understand and maintain.
  - Ensure that the logic behind their use is clear and well-documented.

2.4. Practical Examples: Solving Problems with Conditional Logic and Loops

- Problem-Solving Power:
  - Conditional logic and loops are the workhorses of problem-solving in programming. They enable you to create algorithms that can handle complex tasks and adapt to various inputs.
- Example 1: Finding Prime Numbers:

- Determining whether a number is prime involves checking if it's divisible by any number other than 1 and itself.
- Conditional logic is used to handle edge cases (e.g., numbers less than 2), and a loop is used to iterate through potential divisors.
- Optimization:
  - The loop can be optimized by only checking divisors up to the square root of the number, as any factor greater than the square root would have a corresponding factor less than it.[3]
- Example 2: Calculating Factorials:
  - The factorial of a non-negative integer n is the product of all positive integers less than or equal to n.

- A loop is used to iterate from 1 to n, multiplying each number with the accumulated factorial.
- Example 3: Data Filtering and Processing:
  - Imagine you have a list of student scores, and you need to calculate the average score of students who passed (scores above 60).
  - A loop is used to iterate through the list, and conditional logic is used to filter out failing scores.
  - Real world application:
    - This kind of data filtering and processing is used in many different applications, from financial analysis to scientific research.
- Example 4: Search Algorithms:
  - Loops and conditional logic are the base of search algorithms.

- A linear search will use a loop to iterate through a list until the searched item is found, conditional logic is used to check if the current item is the searched item.[4]
- Binary searches are more efficient, but also rely on loops and conditional logic.
- Key Takeaways:
  - Conditional logic allows you to make decisions based on specific conditions.[5]
  - Loops enable you to automate repetitive tasks.[6]
  - break and continue provide fine-grained control over loop execution.
  - By combining these concepts, you can create powerful and efficient algorithms.

CHAPTER 3

Functions: Building Reusable Code Blocks

Functions are fundamental to writing organized, efficient, and maintainable code.[1] They encapsulate blocks of logic, allowing you to reuse them throughout your program.[2] This modular approach not only saves time and effort but also makes your code easier to understand and debug.[3]

3.1. Defining and Calling Functions: Syntax and Best Practices

- **The Essence of Functions:**
  - At their core, functions are named blocks of code that perform specific tasks.[4] They act as mini-programs within your

larger program, promoting code reusability and reducing redundancy.

- o Functions allow you to break down complex problems into smaller, more manageable parts, making your code more organized and easier to understand.[5]

- **Function Declaration:**
  - o The most common way to define a function is using the function keyword, followed by the function name,[6] a set of parentheses (), and a block of code enclosed in curly braces[7] {}.
  - o **Syntax:**

JavaScript

```javascript
function functionName() {
  // Code to be executed
}
```

* **Example:**

JavaScript

```javascript
function greet() {
  console.log("Hello, World!");
}
```

- **Function Expression:**
  - Another way to define a function is by assigning it to a variable, known as a function expression.[8]
  - **Syntax:**

JavaScript

```javascript
let functionName = function() {
  // Code to be executed
```

```
};
```

* **Example:**

JavaScript

```
let greet = function() {
  console.log("Hello, World!");
};
```

- **Calling Functions:**
  - To execute a function, you need to call it by its name followed by parentheses ().
  - **Example:**

JavaScript

greet(); // Calls the greet function and prints "Hello, World!"

- **Best Practices:**
  - **Descriptive Naming:**
    - Choose function names that clearly indicate their purpose. This makes your code more readable and self-documenting.
  - **Single Responsibility:**
    - Each function should have a single, well-defined responsibility. This promotes modularity and makes your code easier to maintain.
  - **Avoid Global Variables:**
    - Minimize the use of global variables within functions. Instead, rely on function parameters and return values to pass data.

- Code Reusability:
  - Design functions to be reusable. Avoid hardcoding specific values within functions; instead, use parameters to make them more flexible.
- Comments and Documentation:
  - Add comments to your functions to explain their purpose, parameters, and return values. This makes your code easier to understand for yourself and others.
- **Hoisting:**
  - Function declarations are hoisted, meaning they can be called before they are defined in the code.[9] Function expressions are not hoisted.

3.2. Function Parameters and Return Values

- **Function Parameters:**
  - Parameters are variables that receive values when a function is called.[10] They allow you to pass data into a function, making it more versatile.
  - **Syntax:**

JavaScript

```
function functionName(parameter1, parameter2, ...) {
  // Code to be executed
}
```

* **Example:**

JavaScript

```
function greet(name) {
  console.log("Hello, " + name + "!");
}

greet("Alice"); // Calls the greet function
with "Alice" as the parameter.
```

- **Arguments:**
  - When a function is called, the values passed into the function are called arguments.[11]
- **Return Values:**
  - Functions can return values using the return keyword. This allows you to get results back from a function after it has been executed.
  - **Syntax:**

JavaScript

```javascript
function functionName(parameters) {
  // Code to be executed
  return value;
}
```

* **Example:**

JavaScript

```javascript
function add(a, b) {
  return a + b;
}

let sum = add(5, 3); // Calls the add function and stores the result in the sum variable.
console.log(sum); // Output: 8
```

- **Multiple Return Values (Through Objects):**
  - While a function can only return a single value, you can return multiple values by encapsulating them in an object or an array.
  - **Example (Object):**

JavaScript

```javascript
function getPerson(firstName, lastName) {
  return {
    firstName: firstName,
    lastName: lastName,
    fullName: firstName + " " + lastName
  };
}

let person = getPerson("John", "Doe");
console.log(person.fullName);  // Output: John Doe
```

- **Example (Array):**

JavaScript

```
function getCoordinates(){
    return ;
}

let coordinates = getCoordinates();
let x = coordinates[0];
let y = coordinates[1];

console.log(x,y);
```

- **Default Parameters:**
  - ES6 introduced default parameters, which allow you to specify default values for function parameters.[12]
  - **Example:**

JavaScript

```javascript
function greet(name = "Guest") {
  console.log("Hello, " + name + "!");
}

greet(); // Output: Hello, Guest!
greet("Bob"); // Output: Hello, Bob!
```

Functions are essential tools for writing well-structured and maintainable JavaScript code.[13] By mastering function definitions, parameters, and return values, you can create modular and reusable code blocks that enhance the efficiency and clarity of your programs.

3.3. Scope and Closures: Understanding Variable Access

- **Scope: Defining Variable Visibility:**

- Scope determines the accessibility or visibility of variables and functions in different parts of your code.[1] In JavaScript, understanding scope is crucial for preventing naming conflicts and ensuring that variables are used correctly.[2]
- **Global Scope:**
  - Variables declared outside of any function or block have global scope.[3] They can be accessed from anywhere in[4] your code.[5]
  - However, excessive use of global variables can lead to naming collisions and make your code harder to maintain.[6]
- **Function Scope (Legacy):**
  - Variables declared with var inside a function have function scope. They are accessible within the

function and any nested functions.

- var declarations are hoisted, meaning their declarations are moved to the top of the function scope, which can lead to unexpected behavior.

- **Block Scope (Modern):**
  - Variables declared with let or const inside a block (e.g., within an if statement, for loop, or {}) have block scope. They are accessible only within that block and any nested blocks.
  - let and const declarations are also hoisted, but they are not initialized until their declaration is evaluated, leading to a "temporal dead zone"

where they cannot be accessed.

- **Closures: Remembering the Environment:**
  - A closure is a function that remembers its lexical scope, even when it's executed outside of that scope.[7] In other words, a closure can access variables from its outer (enclosing) function, even after the outer function has finished executing.[8]
  - **How Closures Work:**
    - When an inner function is created within an outer function, it forms a closure.[9] This inner function has access to the outer function's variables, even if the outer function returns the inner function.[10]
    - The closure "closes over" the outer function's

variables, preserving their values.[11]

- ○ **Use Cases:**
  - ▪ **Data Privacy:** Closures can be used to create private variables, which are accessible only within the closure.[12]
  - ▪ **Event Handlers:** Closures are commonly used in event handlers to maintain access to variables from the surrounding scope.[13]
  - ▪ **Creating Function Factories:** Closures can be used to create functions that generate other functions with specific configurations.
- • **Example breakdown:**
  - ○ The provided python example, while written in python, clearly demonstrates the concept of

closures. The outer function stores a value, and the inner function, when returned, retains access to that stored value.[14] This is the core concept of closures.

3.4. Arrow Functions: A Modern Approach to Function Definition

- **Concise Syntax:**
  - Arrow functions, introduced in ES6, provide a more concise syntax for defining functions.[15] They are particularly useful for short, one-line functions.
  - **Syntax:**
    - (parameters) => expression
    - If there is only one parameter, the

parentheses can be omitted.[16]
  - If the function body consists of a single expression, the curly braces[17] and return keyword can be omitted.
  - **Example:**
    - const add = (a, b) => a + b;
- **Lexical this:**
  - One of the key differences between arrow functions and traditional functions is how they handle the this keyword.
  - In traditional functions, the value of this depends on how the function is called.
  - Arrow functions do not have their own this binding. They inherit the this value from the surrounding (lexical) scope. This makes them particularly useful for callbacks and event handlers.

- **Implicit Returns:**
  - ○ If the function body consists of a single expression, arrow functions implicitly return the result of that expression.[18]
  - ○ **Example:**
    - ■ const square = (x) => x * x;
- **No** arguments **Object:**
  - ○ Arrow functions do not have their own arguments object. If you need to access the arguments passed to an arrow function, you can use the rest parameter syntax (...args).[19]
- **Use Cases:**
  - ○ **Callbacks:** Arrow functions are commonly used as callbacks in array methods like map, filter, and reduce.
  - ○ **Event Handlers:** They are also used in event handlers to maintain the correct this context.

- ○ **Short, One-Line Functions:** Arrow functions are ideal for defining short, concise functions.[20]
- **Advantages:**
  - ○ Concise syntax.
  - ○ Lexical this binding.
  - ○ Improved code readability.
- **Disadvantages:**
  - ○ Arrow functions cannot be used as constructors.[21]
  - ○ They do not have their own arguments object.
  - ○ Their lexical binding can sometimes lead to unexpected behavior if not understood properly.

By understanding scope, closures, and arrow functions, you can write more efficient, maintainable, and modern JavaScript code.

CHAPTER 4

Working with Arrays: Storing and Manipulating Data Collections

---

Arrays are fundamental data structures in JavaScript, allowing you to store and manage collections of data.[1] They provide a versatile way to organize and manipulate data, making them essential for various programming tasks.[2]

4.1. Creating and Accessing Array Elements

- **Array Creation:**
  - Arrays in JavaScript are ordered lists of values.[3] They can hold values of any data type, including numbers, strings, objects, and even other arrays.[4]

- There are two primary ways to create arrays:
    - **Array Literal Notation:**
        - The most common and concise way to create an array is using square brackets [] and listing the elements inside, separated by commas.
        - **Example:**
            - let myArray = [1, "hello", true, { name: "John" }];
    - **Array Constructor:**
        - You can also create an array using the Array constructor.
        - **Example:**
            - let myArray = new Array(1, "hello", true);

- ○ **Mixed Data Types:**
  - ■ JavaScript arrays are dynamic and can contain elements of different data types within the same array.[5] This flexibility makes them highly versatile.
- • **Accessing Array Elements:**
  - ○ Array elements are accessed using their index, which is a zero-based numerical position.[6]
  - ○ **Index Notation:**
    - ■ To access an element, use the array name followed by the index in square brackets [].
    - ■ **Example:**
      - ■ let myArray = [10, 20, 30];
      - ■ let firstElement = myArray[0];   // firstElement is 10

- let secondElement = myArray[1];   // secondElement is 20

- **Negative Indexing:**
  - While not a standard JavaScript feature, some environments or libraries might provide negative indexing to access elements from the end of the array.

- **Array Length:**
  - The length property of an array returns the number of elements in the array.
  - **Example:**
    - let myArray = [1, 2, 3];
    - console.log(myArray .length); // Output: 3

4.2. Array Methods: push, pop, shift, unshift, and More

- **Modifying Arrays:**
  - JavaScript provides a rich set of built-in methods for modifying arrays, allowing you to add, remove, and manipulate elements efficiently.[7]
- **Adding Elements:**
  - push():
    - The push() method adds one or more elements to the end of an array and returns the new length of the array.
    - **Example:**
      - let numbers = [1, 2, 3];
      - numbers.push(4); // numbers is now [1, 2, 3, 4]
  - unshift():

- The unshift() method adds one or more elements to the beginning of an array and returns the new length of the array.[8]
- **Example:**
  - let numbers = [2, 3, 4];
  - numbers.unshift(1); // numbers is now [1, 2, 3, 4]
  - splice():
    - The splice() method can add or remove elements at any position within the array.
    - This method is extremely powerful.
- **Removing Elements:**
  - pop():
    - The pop() method removes the last element from an array and returns that element.

- **Example:**
  - let numbers = [1, 2, 3];
  - let lastNumber = numbers.pop(); // numbers is now [1, 2], lastNumber is 3
- shift():
  - The shift() method removes the first element from an array and returns that element.
  - **Example:**
    - let numbers = [1, 2, 3];
    - let firstNumber = numbers.shift(); // numbers is now [2, 3], firstNumber is 1
- splice():
  - As stated above, splice can also remove elements.[9]
- **Other Useful Methods:**
  - concat():

- The concat() method creates a new array by merging two or more arrays.
- **Example:**
  - let array1 = [1, 2];
  - let array2 = [3, 4];
  - let combinedArray = array1.concat(array2); // combinedArray is [1, 2, 3, 4]
- slice():
  - The slice() method creates a new array by extracting a portion of an existing array.
  - **Example:**
    - let numbers = [1, 2, 3, 4, 5];
    - let subArray = numbers.slice(1, 4); // subArray is [2, 3, 4]
- indexOf():

- The indexOf() method returns the first index at which a given element can be found in the array, or -1 if it is not[10] present.
    - includes():
        - The includes() method determines whether an array includes a certain value among its entries, returning true or false[11] as appropriate.
    - reverse():
        - The reverse() method reverses the order of the elements in an array.
    - sort():
        - The sort() method sorts the elements of an array in place and returns the sorted array.
- **Iteration:**
    - Arrays are commonly used with loops to iterate through their

elements and perform operations on each element.[12]

- Methods like forEach(), map(), filter(), and reduce() provide powerful ways to iterate and manipulate array data.

Understanding arrays and their methods is essential for any JavaScript developer. They provide a versatile way to store and manipulate data, enabling you to build complex and efficient applications.

4.3. Iterating Through Arrays: forEach, map, filter, and reduce

- **The Power of Iteration:**
  - Iterating through arrays is a fundamental operation in JavaScript. It allows you to process each element in a collection, perform

transformations, filter data, and aggregate values.

- ○ JavaScript provides several built-in methods that simplify array iteration, making your code more concise and readable.[1]
- forEach(): **Executing a Function for Each Element:**
  - ○ The forEach() method executes a provided function once for each array element. It's primarily used for side effects, such as logging or updating external variables.[2]
  - ○ **Syntax:**
    - array.forEach(function(element, index, array) { /* ... */ });
  - ○ **Example:**

JavaScript

```
let numbers = [1, 2, 3, 4, 5];
numbers.forEach(function(number) {
  console.log(number * 2);
});
```

* **Key Points:**
    * `forEach()` does not return a new array.
    * It's suitable for performing actions on each element without creating a new collection.

- map(): **Transforming Array Elements:**
    - The map() method creates a new array by applying a provided function to each element of the original array. It transforms each element and returns a new array with the transformed values.[34]
    - **Syntax:**

- let newArray = array.map(function(element, index, array) { return transformedElement; });
  - **Example:**

JavaScript

```
let numbers = [1, 2, 3, 4, 5];
let doubledNumbers = numbers.map(function(number) {
  return number * 2;
});
console.log(doubledNumbers); // Output: [2, 4, 6, 8, 10]
```

* **Key Points:**
  * `map()` always returns a new array with the same length as the original array.
  * It's ideal for transforming data into a new format.

- filter(): **Selecting Elements Based on a Condition:**
  - The filter() method creates a new array with all elements that pass the test implemented by the provided function.
  - **Syntax:**
    - let newArray = array.filter(function(element, index, array) { return condition; });
  - **Example:**

JavaScript

```javascript
let numbers = [1, 2, 3, 4, 5];
let evenNumbers = numbers.filter(function(number) {
  return number % 2 === 0;
});
console.log(evenNumbers); // Output: [2, 4]
```

* **Key Points:**
  * `filter()` returns a new array containing only the elements that satisfy the condition.
  * It's useful for extracting subsets of data based on specific criteria.

- reduce(): **Aggregating Array Elements:**
  - The reduce() method applies a function against an accumulator and each element in the array (from left to right) to reduce it to[5] a single value.
  - **Syntax:**
    - let result = array.reduce(function(accumulator, currentValue, currentIndex, array) { return accumulatedValue; }, initialValue);
  - **Example:**

JavaScript

```javascript
let numbers = [1, 2, 3, 4, 5];
let sum = numbers.reduce(function(accumulator, currentValue) {
  return accumulator + currentValue;
}, 0);
console.log(sum); // Output: 15
```

* **Key Points:**
    * `reduce()` returns a single value.
    * It's powerful for aggregating data, such as summing numbers, calculating averages, or combining strings.
    * Initial value is optional.

- **Chaining Methods:**
    - These array methods can be chained together to perform complex data manipulations in a single, concise expression.[6]

JavaScript

```
let numbers = [1, 2, 3, 4, 5];
let result = numbers
 .filter(number => number % 2 === 0)
 .map(number => number * 3)
  .reduce((accumulator, currentValue) =>
accumulator + currentValue, 0);
console.log(result); // Output: 18
```

4.4. Multidimensional Arrays: Organizing Complex Data

- **Arrays of Arrays:**
  - ○ Multidimensional arrays are arrays that contain other arrays as elements.[7] They allow you to represent complex data

structures, such as matrices, tables, or grids.

- ○ **Example:**

JavaScript

```
let matrix = [
  [1, 2, 3],
  [4, 5, 6],
  [7, 8, 9]
];
```

- **Accessing Elements:**
  - ○ To access an element in a multidimensional array, you use multiple index notations, one for each dimension.
  - ○ **Example:**

JavaScript

```
let element = matrix[1][2]; // element is 6
```

- **Iterating Through Multidimensional Arrays:**
  - You can use nested loops to iterate through multidimensional arrays and access each element.[8]
  - **Example:**

JavaScript

```
for (let i = 0; i < matrix.length; i++) {
 for (let j = 0; j < matrix[i].length; j++) {
  console.log(matrix[i][j]);
 }
}
```

- **Use Cases:**

- **Game Development:** Multidimensional arrays are used to represent game boards, tile maps, and other game data.[9]
- **Data Analysis:** They are used to store and manipulate tabular data, such as spreadsheets or databases.
- **Image Processing:** Multidimensional arrays can represent pixel data for images.
- **Representing Coordinates:** useful for storing coordinates in a 2d or 3d space.

By mastering array iteration and multidimensional arrays, you can effectively manage and manipulate complex data structures in your JavaScript applications.

CHAPTER 5

Objects: Real-World   Representing Entities

Objects are fundamental to JavaScript, serving as versatile containers for data and functionality.[1] They allow you to model real-world entities with properties and behaviors, making your code more intuitive and organized.[2]

5.1. Creating and Accessing Object Properties

- **The Essence of Objects:**
  - Objects are collections of key-value pairs, where keys are strings (or symbols) and values can be any data type, including numbers, strings, booleans, arrays, and even other objects.[3]

- They allow you to group related data and functionality together, creating self-contained units of code.
- **Object Creation:**
  - There are several ways to create objects in JavaScript:
    - **Object Literal Notation:**
      - The most common and concise way to create an object is using curly braces {} and defining key-value pairs inside.
      - **Syntax:**

JavaScript

let myObject = {

```
  key1: value1,
  key2: value2,
  // ...
};
```

* **Example:**

JavaScript

```
let person = {
  firstName: "John",
  lastName: "Doe",
  age: 30,
  city: "New York"
};
```

* **Object Constructor:**
    * You can also create objects using the `Object` constructor.
    * **Syntax:**

JavaScript

```
let myObject = new Object();
myObject.key1 = value1;
myObject.key2 = value2;
```

* **Example:**

JavaScript

```
let person = new Object();
person.firstName = "John";
person.lastName = "Doe";
person.age = 30;
person.city = "New York";
```

* **Factory Functions:**
    * Factory functions are functions that return objects.

* **Example:**

JavaScript

```javascript
function createPerson(firstName, lastName, age, city) {
  return {
    firstName: firstName,
    lastName: lastName,
    age: age,
    city: city
  };
}

let person1 = createPerson("John", "Doe", 30, "New York");
```

* **Constructor Functions (Classes):**
    * Constructor functions, or classes in ES6, provide a blueprint for creating objects with similar properties and methods.
    * **Example:**

JavaScript

```javascript
function Person(firstName, lastName, age, city) {
  this.firstName = firstName;
  this.lastName = lastName;
  this.age = age;
  this.city = city;
}

let person1 = new Person("John", "Doe", 30, "New York");
```

- **Accessing Object Properties:**
  - Object properties can be accessed using two primary methods:
    - **Dot Notation:**
      - Use the object name followed by a dot .

and the property
name.

- **Example:**

JavaScript

```
console.log(person.firstName); // Output:
John
```

* **Bracket Notation:**
    * Use the object name followed by
square brackets `[]` and the property name
as a string.
    * **Example:**

JavaScript

```
console.log(person["lastName"]); // Output:
Doe
```

* **Dynamic Property Access:**
  * Bracket notation is particularly useful for accessing properties dynamically, where the property name is stored in a variable.
  * **Example:**

JavaScript

```
let propertyName = "age";
console.log(person[propertyName]);     //
Output: 30
```

- **Adding and Modifying Properties:**
  - You can add new properties to an object or modify existing properties using dot or bracket notation.[4]
  - **Example:**

JavaScript

```
person.job = "Developer"; // Adding a new property
person.age = 31; // Modifying an existing property
```

- **Deleting Properties:**
  - The delete operator can be used to remove properties from an object.
  - **Example:**

JavaScript

```
delete person.city; // Removes the city property
```

5.2. Object Methods: Functions Within Objects

- **Methods as Object Behaviors:**
  - Methods are functions that are associated with an object.[5] They define the behaviors or actions that an object can perform.[6]
  - Methods are defined as properties whose values are functions.[7]
- **Defining Methods:**
  - You can define methods within an object literal or using dot or bracket notation.[8]
  - **Example:**

JavaScript

```
let person = {
 firstName: "John",
 lastName: "Doe",
```

```javascript
age: 30,
fullName: function() {
        return this.firstName + " " +
this.lastName;
 }
};
```

- **Calling Methods:**
  - Methods are called using dot or bracket notation, just like accessing properties.
  - **Example:**

JavaScript

```javascript
console.log(person.fullName()); // Output:
John Doe
```

- **The this Keyword:**

- The this keyword refers to the object that the method is called on. It allows methods to access and manipulate the object's properties.
- **Example:**

JavaScript

```
let car = {
  make: "Toyota",
  model: "Camry",
  start: function() {
    console.log("Starting the " + this.make + " " + this.model);
  }
};

car.start(); // Output: Starting the Toyota Camry
```

- **Arrow Functions and** this**:**
  - Arrow functions do not have their own this binding. They inherit the this value from the surrounding (lexical) scope. This can lead to unexpected behavior if used as object methods.
  - It's generally recommended to use traditional function expressions for object methods.
- **Use Cases:**
  - **Modeling Real-World Entities:** Objects are used to represent real-world entities, such as people, cars, or products.[9]
  - **Organizing Code:** Objects help organize code by grouping related data and functionality together.
  - **Creating Complex Data Structures:** Objects can be nested within other objects to create complex data structures.[10]

- **Implementing Object-Oriented Programming (OOP) Concepts:** Objects are fundamental to OOP concepts like encapsulation, inheritance, and polymorphism.

By mastering object creation, property access, and methods, you can effectively model real-world entities and create complex data structures in your JavaScript applications.

5.3. Object Literals and Constructors

* **Object Literals: Simplicity and Directness**
  * Object literals, denoted by curly braces `{}`, provide a straightforward and concise way to create objects. They are ideal for

creating single instances of objects with specific properties and methods.
   * **Advantages:**

   * **Readability:** Object literals are highly readable and easy to understand, making them ideal for small, self-contained objects.

   * **Simplicity:** They require minimal syntax, allowing you to create objects quickly and efficiently.

   * **Flexibility:** You can easily add, modify, or delete properties and methods within an object literal.

   * **Use Cases:**

   * Creating configuration objects with specific settings.

   * Defining data structures for storing and manipulating data.

   * Creating single instances of objects with unique properties.

   * **Example:**

```javascript
let book = {
```

```
  title: "The JavaScript Guide",
  author: "Jane Smith",
  pages: 300,
  read: function() {
    console.log("Reading " + this.title);
  }
};
```

* **Constructor Functions: Blueprints for Objects**
  * Constructor functions, or classes in ES6, provide a blueprint for creating multiple objects with similar properties and methods. They are essential for creating reusable object structures.
    * **How Constructors Work:**
      * Constructor functions are called using the `new` keyword, which creates a new object and sets the `this` keyword to refer to that object.
      * Properties and methods are added to the object using the `this` keyword.

* Constructor functions typically have names that start with a capital letter, following the convention for classes.
   * **Advantages:**
         * **Reusability:** Constructor functions allow you to create multiple objects with the same structure, reducing code duplication.
         * **Encapsulation:** They can be used to encapsulate data and functionality within objects, promoting modularity and maintainability.
         * **Inheritance (with Prototypes or Classes):** Constructor functions, or classes, are the base of javascripts inheritance model.
   * **Use Cases:**
         * Creating multiple instances of objects with similar properties, such as users, products, or employees.
         * Implementing object-oriented programming (OOP) concepts.
         * Creating custom data types with specific behaviors.

* **Example:**

```javascript
function Book(title, author, pages) {
  this.title = title;
  this.author = author;
  this.pages = pages;
  this.read = function() {
    console.log("Reading " + this.title);
  };
}

let book1 = new Book("The JavaScript Guide", "Jane Smith", 300);
let book2 = new Book("Eloquent JavaScript", "Marijn Haverbeke", 472);
```

* **Key Differences:**
  * Object literals create single instances, while constructor functions create blueprints for multiple instances.
  * Object literals are simpler and more direct, while constructor functions offer greater reusability and encapsulation.

5.4. JSON: JavaScript Object Notation for Data Exchange

* **The Power of JSON:**

  * JSON (JavaScript Object Notation) is a lightweight data-interchange format that is easy for humans to read and write and easy for machines to parse and generate.

  * It is widely used for transmitting data between web applications and servers, as well as for storing and configuring data.

* **JSON Syntax:**

  * JSON syntax is based on JavaScript object literals, but it has some important differences:

    * Keys must be enclosed in double quotes.

    * Values can be strings, numbers, booleans, arrays, objects, or `null`.

    * JSON does not support functions or `undefined`.

  * **Example:**

```json
{
  "firstName": "John",
  "lastName": "Doe",
  "age": 30,
  "address": {
    "street": "123 Main St",
    "city": "Anytown",
    "country": "USA"
  },
  "phoneNumbers": ["555-1234", "555-5678"]
}
```

* **`JSON.stringify()`** and `JSON.parse()`:**
    * JavaScript provides two built-in methods for working with JSON:
    * **`JSON.stringify()`:** Converts a JavaScript object or value to a JSON string.
    * **`JSON.parse()`:** Parses a JSON string and converts it to a JavaScript object or value.

* **Example:**

```javascript
let person = {
  firstName: "John",
  lastName: "Doe",
  age: 30
};

let jsonString = JSON.stringify(person);
console.log(jsonString); // Output: {"firstName":"John","lastName":"Doe","age":30}

let parsedPerson = JSON.parse(jsonString);
console.log(parsedPerson.firstName); // Output: John
```

* **Use Cases:**
    * **Web APIs:** JSON is the standard format for data exchange in web APIs.

* **Configuration Files:** JSON is used to store configuration settings for applications.
* **Data Storage:** JSON is used to store data in databases and files.
* **Interoperability:** JSON's platform-independent nature makes it ideal for data exchange between different programming languages and systems.

By understanding object literals, constructors, and JSON, you can effectively create, manipulate, and exchange data in your JavaScript applications.

CHAPTER 6

The Document Object Model (DOM): Interacting with Web Pages

The DOM is a crucial concept in web development, serving as the interface between JavaScript and the structure of HTML documents.[1] It allows you to dynamically manipulate web page content, style, and behavior.[2]

6.1. Understanding the DOM Structure

- **The DOM as a Tree Structure:**
  - The DOM represents an HTML or XML document as a tree-like structure, where each element, attribute, and text node is a node in the tree.[3]

- The root node of the tree is the document object, which represents the entire HTML document.
- Each HTML element is represented as an element node, with properties and methods for accessing and manipulating its content and attributes.[4]
- Text content within elements is represented as text nodes.[5]
- Attributes of elements are represented as attribute nodes.

- **Nodes and Relationships:**
  - **Parent Nodes:** Nodes can have parent nodes, which are the nodes directly above them in the tree hierarchy.[6]
  - **Child Nodes:** Nodes can have child nodes, which are the nodes directly below them in the tree hierarchy.[7]

- ○ **Sibling Nodes:** Nodes that share the same parent node are sibling nodes.[8]
- ○ **Document Object:** The document object is the root of the DOM tree. It provides methods for accessing and manipulating the entire document.[9]
- **HTML to DOM:**
  - ○ When a web browser loads an HTML document, it parses the HTML and constructs the DOM tree.[10]
  - ○ The browser interprets the HTML tags and attributes and creates corresponding nodes in the DOM tree.[11]
  - ○ JavaScript can then access and manipulate these nodes to dynamically modify the web page.[12]
- **Visualizing the DOM:**

- Browsers' developer tools provide a visual representation of the DOM tree, allowing you to inspect the structure of web pages.[13]
- The "Elements" tab in developer tools displays the HTML elements and their relationships in the DOM tree.

- **Key DOM Properties:**
  - nodeType: Indicates the type of node (e.g., element node, text node, attribute node).[14]
  - nodeName: Returns the name of the node (e.g., tag name for element nodes).[15]
  - nodeValue: Returns the value of the node (e.g., text content for text nodes).[16]
  - parentNode: Returns the parent node of the node.[17]
  - childNodes: Returns a list of child nodes of the node.[18]

- firstChild: Returns the first child node of the node.[19]
- lastChild: Returns the last child node of the node.[20]
- nextSibling: Returns the next sibling node of the node.[21]
- previousSibling: Returns the previous sibling node of the node.

6.2. Selecting DOM Elements: getElementById, querySelector, and More

- **Accessing Elements:**
  - To manipulate DOM elements, you first need to select them using JavaScript.
  - The document object provides several methods for selecting elements based on their ID, class, tag name, or other criteria.

- getElementById():
    - The getElementById() method selects an element by its ID attribute.
    - IDs must be unique within an HTML document.[22]
    - **Syntax:**
        - document.getElementById ("elementId");
    - **Example:**

JavaScript

```
let myElement = document.getElementById("myDiv");
```

- getElementsByClassName():
    - The getElementsByClassName() method selects all elements with a specified class name.

- It returns an HTMLCollection, which is an array-like object containing the selected elements.[23]
- **Syntax:**
  - document.getElementsBy ClassName("className");
- **Example:**

JavaScript

```
let elements = document.getElementsByClassName("myClass");
```

- getElementsByTagName():
  - The getElementsByTagName() method selects all elements with a specified tag name.
  - It returns an HTMLCollection.
  - **Syntax:**

- document.getElementsByT
  agName("tagName");
  - **Example:**

JavaScript

let paragraphs =
document.getElementsByTagName("p");

- querySelector():
  - The querySelector() method
    selects the first element that
    matches a specified CSS selector.
  - It provides a more flexible and
    powerful way to select elements
    using CSS syntax.
  - **Syntax:**
    - document.querySelector("
      selector");
  - **Example:**

JavaScript

```
        let      myElement     =
document.querySelector("#myDiv");      //
Selects by ID
        let    firstParagraph     =
document.querySelector("p"); // Selects the
first paragraph
            let     firstClass     =
document.querySelector(".myClass");      //
Selects the first element of class myClass
```

- querySelectorAll():
  - The querySelectorAll() method selects all elements that match a specified CSS selector.
  - It returns a NodeList, which is an array-like object containing the selected elements.[24]
  - **Syntax:**
    - document.querySelectorAl l("selector");
  - **Example:**

JavaScript

```
            let        allParagraphs        =
document.querySelectorAll("p");
            let        allClasses        =
document.querySelectorAll(".myClass");
```

- **Traversal:**
    - Once you have selected an element, you can traverse the DOM tree using properties like parentNode, childNodes, nextSibling, and previousSibling to navigate to related elements.

By understanding the DOM structure and mastering element selection, you can effectively manipulate web page content and create interactive and dynamic web applications.[25]

6.3. Modifying DOM Elements: Changing Content and Attributes

- **Dynamic Web Pages:**
  - The ability to modify DOM elements dynamically is what makes web pages interactive. JavaScript empowers you to change the content, style, and attributes of elements in response to user actions or other events.
- **Changing Content:**
  - textContent:
    - The textContent property sets or returns the text content of a node and its descendants.
    - It's useful for replacing the entire text content of an element.
    - It is important to note that textContent will not render HTML.[1]

■ Example:

JavaScript

```
        let  myElement  =
document.getElementById("myDiv");
    myElement.textContent = "New text
content";
```

* **`innerHTML`:**
    * The `innerHTML` property sets or returns the HTML content of an element.
    * It allows you to insert HTML markup into an element, which the browser will parse and render.
    * **Example:**

JavaScript

```javascript
let myElement =
document.getElementById("myDiv");
    myElement.innerHTML =
"<strong>Bold    text</strong>    and
<em>italic text</em>";
```

* **Creating and Appending Elements:**
    * You can create new DOM elements using the `document.createElement()` method.
    * You can append these elements to the DOM tree using methods like `appendChild()`, `insertBefore()`, and `replaceChild()`.
    * **Example:**

JavaScript

```javascript
    let newParagraph =
document.createElement("p");
    newParagraph.textContent = "This is a
new paragraph.";
```

```
document.body.appendChild(newParagraph
);
```

- **Changing Attributes:**
  - setAttribute():
    - The setAttribute() method sets the value of an attribute on a specified element.
    - **Example:**

JavaScript

```
let    myImage    =
document.getElementById("myImage");
    myImage.setAttribute("src",
"new-image.jpg");
    myImage.setAttribute("alt", "A new
image");
```

* **`getAttribute()`:**
    * The `getAttribute()` method returns the value of a specified attribute on the element.
    * **Example:**

JavaScript

```
let imageSource = myImage.getAttribute("src");
console.log(imageSource);
```

* **`removeAttribute()`:**
    * The `removeAttribute()` method removes a specified attribute from an element.
    * **Example:**

JavaScript

myImage.removeAttribute("alt");

* **`classList`:**
    * The `classList` property provides methods for manipulating the class attributes of an element.
    * **`add()`:** Adds a class.
    * **`remove()`:** Removes a class.
    * **`toggle()`:** Toggles a class.
    * **`contains()`:** Checks if a class exists.
    * **Example:**

JavaScript

```
let myElement = document.getElementById("myDiv");
myElement.classList.add("highlight");

myElement.classList.remove("old-class");
myElement.classList.toggle("active");
```

```
if(myElement.classList.contains("highlight"
)) {
        console.log("the element has the class
Highlight");
    }
```

- **Changing Styles:**
  - The style property allows you to modify the inline styles of an element.
  - **Example:**

JavaScript

```
            let myElement =
document.getElementById("myDiv");
        myElement.style.backgroundColor =
"lightblue";
    myElement.style.color = "darkblue";
    myElement.style.padding = "10px";
```

6.4. Handling Events: Responding to User Interactions

- **Event-Driven Programming:**
  - Event handling is a fundamental concept in web development.[2] It allows your JavaScript code to respond to user actions and other events that occur in the browser.
- **Event Listeners:**
  - Event listeners are functions that are executed when a specific event occurs on an element.[3]
  - The addEventListener() method is used to attach event listeners to elements.
  - **Syntax:**

JavaScript

```
element.addEventListener(eventType,
listenerFunction);
```

* **Example:**

JavaScript

```
let myButton =
document.getElementById("myButton");
myButton.addEventListener("click",
function() {
console.log("Button clicked!");
});
```

- **Common Event Types:**
  - click: Occurs when an element is clicked.[4]

- o mouseover: Occurs when the mouse pointer moves over an element.[5]
- o mouseout: Occurs when the mouse pointer moves out of an element.[6]
- o keydown: Occurs when a[7] key is pressed down.[8]
- o keyup: Occurs when a key is released.[9]
- o submit: Occurs when a form is submitted.[10]
- o load: Occurs when a[11] page or element has finished loading.[12]
- o change: Occurs when the value of an input element changes.[13]
- **Event Objects:**
  - o When an event occurs, an event object is created.[14] This object contains information about the event, such as the target element, the event type, and any other relevant data.[15]
  - o **Example:**

JavaScript

```
myButton.addEventListener("click",
function(event) {
    console.log("Event  target:",
event.target);
    console.log("Event type:", event.type);
});
```

- **Event Propagation:**
  - Events can propagate through the DOM tree in two phases:[16]
    - **Capturing Phase:** The event travels from the root of the DOM tree down to the target element.[17]
    - **Bubbling Phase:** The event travels from the target element up to the root of the DOM tree.[18]
  -
  - You can control the event propagation using the third

argument of the addEventListener() method.

- **Preventing Default Behavior:**
  - The preventDefault() method can be used to prevent the default behavior of an event, such as preventing a form from submitting or preventing a link from navigating.
  - **Example:**

JavaScript

```
let myLink = document.getElementById("myLink");
myLink.addEventListener("click", function(event) {
event.preventDefault();
console.log("Link clicked, but navigation prevented.");
});
```

By mastering DOM manipulation and event handling, you can create dynamic and interactive web pages that respond to user actions and provide a rich and engaging user experience.

CHAPTER 7

Events and Event Handling: Making Web Pages Interactive

Events are the lifeblood of interactive web applications. They represent actions or occurrences that happen in the browser, such as user interactions, page loading, and network responses. Event handling allows you to write JavaScript code that responds to these events, making your web pages dynamic and engaging.

7.1. Common Event Types: click, mouseover, keydown, and More

- **The Essence of Events:**
  - ○ Events are signals that something has happened in the browser. They can be triggered by user actions, such as clicking a button or typing in a text field,

or by browser actions, such as a page finishing loading or a network request completing.

○ Understanding the different types of events and how to handle them is crucial for creating interactive web applications.

- **Common Event Types:**
  ○ click:
    ■ Occurs when the user clicks on an element.
    ■ It's one of the most common events and is used for triggering actions when a button, link, or other interactive element is clicked.
  ○ mouseover:
    ■ Occurs when the mouse pointer moves over an element.
    ■ It's often used for displaying tooltips,

highlighting elements, or triggering animations.

- mouseout:
  - Occurs when the mouse pointer moves out of an element.
  - It's used to reverse the effects of mouseover or to hide tooltips.
- keydown:
  - Occurs when a key is pressed down.
  - It's used for capturing keyboard input, such as typing in a text field or triggering keyboard shortcuts.
- keyup:
  - Occurs when a key is released.
  - It's used to capture keyboard input and to perform actions when a key is released.

- submit:
  - Occurs when a form is submitted.
  - It's used to validate form data and to send the form data to a server.
- load:
  - Occurs when a page or element has finished loading.
  - It's used to perform actions after a page or element has loaded, such as initializing variables or setting up event listeners.
- change:
  - Occurs when the value of an input element changes.
  - It's used to capture changes in form elements, such as text fields, checkboxes, and select boxes.
- focus:

- Occurs when an element gains focus (e.g., when a text field is clicked).
  - blur:
    - Occurs when an element loses focus.
  - scroll:
    - Occurs when the user scrolls the page.
  - resize:
    - Occurs when the browser window is resized.
  - touchstart, touchmove, touchend:
    - Occur on touch-enabled devices.
- **Event Objects:**
  - When an event occurs, an event object is created. This object contains information about the event, such as the target element, the event type, and any other relevant data.

- You can access the event object in the event listener function.
- **Example:**

JavaScript

```
        myButton.addEventListener("click",
function(event) {
                console.log("Event    target:",
event.target);
    console.log("Event type:", event.type);
  });
```

7.2. Adding and Removing Event Listeners

- **Attaching Event Listeners:**
  - Event listeners are functions that are executed when a specific event occurs on an element.
  - The addEventListener() method is used to attach event listeners to elements.

○ **Syntax:**

JavaScript

    element.addEventListener(eventType, listenerFunction, useCapture);

* **`eventType`:** The type of event to listen for (e.g., "click", "mouseover").
* **`listenerFunction`:** The function to be executed when the event occurs.
* **`useCapture` (optional):** A boolean value that specifies whether to use event capturing or event bubbling.
  * `true`: Use capturing.
  * `false` (default): Use bubbling.
* **Example:**

JavaScript

```
        let        myButton        =
document.getElementById("myButton");
        myButton.addEventListener("click",
function() {
    console.log("Button clicked!");
    });
```

- **Removing Event Listeners:**
    - The   removeEventListener()
      method is used to remove event
      listeners from elements.
    - **Syntax:**

JavaScript

```
    element.removeEventListener(eventType,
listenerFunction, useCapture);
```

* **Important:**

* You must provide the same `listenerFunction` that you used when adding the event listener. Anonymous functions cannot be removed.
* The `useCapture` parameter must also match the value used when adding the event listener.
* **Example:**

JavaScript

```
function handleClick() {
  console.log("Button clicked!");
}


myButton.addEventListener("click", handleClick);
myButton.removeEventListener("click", handleClick);
```

- **Event Propagation:**

- Events can propagate through the DOM tree in two phases:
  - **Capturing Phase:** The event travels from the root of the DOM tree down to the target element.
  - **Bubbling Phase:** The event travels from the target element up to the root of the DOM tree.
- You can control the event propagation using the third argument of the addEventListener() method.
- **Preventing Default Behavior:**
  - The preventDefault() method can be used to prevent the default behavior of an event, such as preventing a form from submitting or preventing a link from navigating.
  - **Example:**

JavaScript

```
            let       myLink      =
document.getElementById("myLink");
        myLink.addEventListener("click",
function(event) {
   event.preventDefault();
   console.log("Link clicked, but navigation
prevented.");
   });
```

By understanding event types and mastering event handling, you can create dynamic and interactive web pages that respond to user actions and provide a rich and engaging user experience.

7.3. Event Propagation: Bubbling and Capturing

- **Understanding the Flow of Events:**

- Event propagation describes the order in which event handlers are called when an event occurs on a nested element. It's a fundamental concept for understanding how events behave in the DOM.
- When an event occurs on an element, it doesn't just trigger the event handler on that element. It also triggers event handlers on its ancestor elements, following a specific path through the DOM tree.[1]

- **The Two Phases:**
  - **Capturing Phase:**
    - In the capturing phase, the event travels from the root of the DOM tree down to the target element.[2]
    - Event handlers registered for the capturing phase are executed before the event

reaches the target element.[3]

- This phase allows you to intercept events before they reach their intended target.[4]

- **Bubbling Phase:**
  - In the bubbling phase, the event travels from the target element up to the root of the DOM tree.
  - Event handlers registered for the bubbling phase are executed after the event has been handled by the target element.
  - This is the most common and default phase of event propagation.[5]

- **How it Works in Practice:**
  - Imagine you have a nested structure like this:

HTML

```
<div id="outer">
  <div id="inner">
              <button id="target">Click Me</button>
  </div>
</div>
```

* If you click the "Click Me" button, the following happens:
    * **Capturing Phase:**
            * The event starts at the `window` object.
            * It travels down to the `document` object.
            * It continues down to the `html` element.
        * It reaches the `body` element.
        * It then goes to the `outer` `div`, then the `inner` `div`.
    * **Target Phase:**

* The event reaches the target element, the `button`.

   * **Bubbling Phase:**

      * The event travels back up the DOM tree, from the `button` to the `inner` `div`, then the `outer` `div`, then the `body`, then the `html`, then the `document`, and finally the `window`.

- **Controlling Propagation:**
   - addEventListener()**'s** useCapture **Parameter:**
      - The third parameter of the addEventListener() method, useCapture, determines whether the event handler is registered for the capturing or bubbling phase.
      - true for capturing, false (or omitted) for bubbling.
   - event.stopPropagation()**:**

170

- The event.stopPropagation() method stops the event from propagating further in either the capturing or bubbling phase.
- This allows you to prevent parent elements from receiving the event.
  - event.stopImmediatePropagation():
    - This method will stop the event from continuing through the rest of the event listeners on the current element, and will also stop the event from bubbling or capturing.[6]
- **Use Cases:**
  - **Event Delegation:**
    - Event delegation is a technique where you attach a single event listener to a parent

element instead of attaching event listeners to each child element.[7]

- This can improve performance and reduce memory usage, especially when dealing with a large number of child elements.[8]
- Event delegation relies on event bubbling to capture events from child elements.[9]
  - **Overlapping Elements:**
    - Event propagation can be used to handle events on overlapping elements.
    - By using the capturing or bubbling phase, you can control which element receives the event.[10]
- **Practical application of capturing:**
  - A website could use capturing to log all click events that occur on

the page. This would be done by attaching an event listener to the window object with the useCapture parameter set to true.

7.4. Practical Event-Driven Applications

- **Creating Interactive Forms:**
  - ○ Event listeners can be used to validate form data in real-time as the user types, providing instant feedback and improving the user experience.[11]
  - ○ For example, you can use the keyup event to check the validity of an email address or password.
- **Building Dynamic UI Elements:**
  - ○ Event handling is essential for creating dynamic UI elements,

such as dropdown menus, tooltips, and modal dialogs.[12]

- You can use events like mouseover, mouseout, and click to control the visibility and behavior of these elements.

- **Implementing Drag-and-Drop Functionality:**
  - Drag-and-drop functionality relies heavily on event handling.[13]
  - You can use events like mousedown, mousemove, and mouseup to track the mouse movements and update the position of the dragged element.

- **Developing Interactive Games:**
  - Event handling is crucial for creating interactive games.
  - You can use events like keydown, keyup, and click to capture user input and control the game's logic.

- **Real-Time Data Updates:**

○ Using Websockets, and event listeners, you can create real time updates to web pages.[14]

○ When data is changed on a server, that change can be sent to all connected clients, and the clients can then update their web page with the new information.

- **Example: A Simple To-Do List:**

  ○ You can create a simple to-do list application using event handling.

    ■ Use an input field and a button to add new tasks.

    ■ Use the click event to add a task to the list.

    ■ Use the click event on each task to mark it as completed or delete it.

- **Example: Image Gallery:**

  ○ An image gallery could use event listeners to change the displayed

image when a user clicks on a thumbnail.
- ○ Mouseover events could be used to display image titles.
- **Key Considerations:**
  - ○ **Performance:** Avoid attaching too many event listeners, as this can impact performance.
  - ○ **Memory Leaks:** Be sure to remove event listeners when they are no longer needed to prevent memory leaks.
  - ○ **Cross-Browser Compatibility:** Test your event handling code in different browsers to ensure compatibility.
  - ○ **User Experience:** Design your event handling logic to provide a smooth and intuitive user experience.

By mastering event propagation and building practical event-driven applications, you can create dynamic and engaging web experiences that are both functional and user-friendly.

CHAPTER 8

Asynchronous JavaScript: Handling Time-Consuming Operations

Asynchronous JavaScript is essential for handling operations that might take a significant amount of time to complete, such as network requests, file I/O, or complex calculations.[1] It allows your code to continue executing while waiting for these operations to finish, preventing the browser from freezing and providing a smoother user experience.[2]

8.1. Understanding Asynchronous Programming

- **The Problem of Blocking Operations:**
  - In synchronous programming, code executes sequentially, one

line after another.[3] If a line of code takes a long time to execute, the entire program will be blocked until that line finishes.[4]

- This can be a major problem in web applications, where long-running operations can cause the browser to freeze and become unresponsive.

- **The Solution: Asynchronous Programming:**
  - Asynchronous programming allows your code to execute non-sequentially.[5] When an asynchronous operation is started, the program doesn't wait for it to finish. Instead, it continues executing the next lines of code.
  - When the asynchronous operation is complete, a callback function is executed to handle the result.[6]

- This allows your code to remain responsive, even when performing time-consuming tasks.[7]
- **The Event Loop:**
  - JavaScript uses an event loop to manage asynchronous operations.[8]
  - The event loop continuously checks the call stack and the task queue.[9]
  - When the call stack is empty, the event loop takes the first[10] task from the task queue and pushes[11] it onto the call stack.[12]
  - This allows asynchronous operations to be executed without blocking the main thread.[13]
- **Key Concepts:**
  - **Non-Blocking:** Asynchronous operations do not block the execution of other code.

- ○ **Callbacks:** Functions that are executed when an asynchronous operation completes.
- ○ **Event Loop:** The mechanism that manages asynchronous operations in JavaScript.
- ○ **Task Queue:** A queue that holds tasks to be executed by the event loop.[14]
- **Use Cases:**
  - ○ **Network Requests:** Fetching data from a server.[15]
  - ○ **File I/O:** Reading or writing files.[16]
  - ○ **Timers:** Setting timeouts or intervals.
  - ○ **User Interactions:** Handling user input without blocking the main thread.[17]
  - ○ **Animations:** Creating smooth animations without blocking the main thread.[18]

8.2. Callbacks: The Traditional Approach

- **Callbacks as Function Arguments:**
  - Callbacks are functions that are passed as arguments to other functions.[19]
  - When the outer function completes its task, it calls the callback function to handle the result.
  - This allows you to define custom logic for handling asynchronous operations.
- **Example:** setTimeout():
  - The setTimeout() function is a common example of using callbacks.
  - It allows you to execute a function after a specified delay.
  - **Syntax:**

JavaScript

```
setTimeout(callbackFunction, delay);
```

* **Example:**

JavaScript

```
console.log("Before timeout");
setTimeout(function() {
  console.log("Timeout completed");
}, 2000);
console.log("After timeout");
```

* **Output:**

```
Before timeout
After timeout
Timeout completed (after 2 seconds)
```

- **Example: Asynchronous Data Fetching (Simulated):**

JavaScript

```javascript
function fetchData(callback) {
  setTimeout(function() {
    let data = "Data fetched successfully";
    callback(data);
  }, 1000);
}

fetchData(function(result) {
  console.log(result);
});

console.log("Fetching data...");
```

* **Output:**

Fetching data...
Data fetched successfully (after 1 second)

- **The Problem of Callback Hell:**
  - When dealing with multiple asynchronous operations, callbacks can become nested, leading to a situation known as "callback hell" or "pyramid of doom."[20]
  - This makes code difficult to read, write, and maintain.
  - **Example (Callback Hell):**
-

JavaScript

```javascript
asyncOperation1(function(result1) {
                asyncOperation2(result1,
function(result2) {
                asyncOperation3(result2,
function(result3) {
```

```
    // ... more nested callbacks
  });
 });
});
```

- **Solutions to Callback Hell:**
  - **Named Functions:** Break down the callback functions into separate, named functions.
  - **Modularization:** Organize your code into smaller, reusable modules.
  - **Promises:** Use promises to handle asynchronous operations in a more structured and readable way.[21]
  - **Async/Await:** Use async/await syntax to write asynchronous code that looks like synchronous code.

By understanding asynchronous programming and mastering callbacks, you can create responsive and efficient web applications that handle time-consuming operations without blocking the main thread. However, it is essential to be aware of the callback hell issue and to use modern techniques like promises and async/await to write cleaner and more maintainable asynchronous code.

8.3. Promises: A Cleaner Way to Handle Asynchronous Code

- **The Promise of Promises:**
  - Promises are objects that represent the eventual completion (or failure) of an asynchronous operation and its resulting value.[1]
  - They provide[2] a structured and readable way to handle asynchronous code, addressing

the issues of callback hell and improving code maintainability.[3]

- **Promise States:**
  - A Promise has three states:[4]
    - **Pending:** The initial state, neither fulfilled nor rejected.[5]
    - **Fulfilled (Resolved):** The operation completed successfully.
    - **Rejected:** The operation failed.[6]
  -

- **Creating Promises:**
  - Promises are created using the Promise constructor, which takes a function called the "executor."
  - The executor function takes two arguments: resolve and reject.
  - resolve is called when the operation succeeds, and reject is called when it fails.
  - **Syntax:**

JavaScript

```
let myPromise = new Promise((resolve,
reject) => {
// Asynchronous operation here
if (/* success */) {
    resolve(value); // Resolve with the
result value
} else {
    reject(error); // Reject with an error
object
}
});
```

- **Consuming Promises:**
  - Promises are consumed using the then() and catch() methods.
  - then() is called when the Promise is fulfilled, and catch() is called when it is rejected.
  - **Syntax:**

JavaScript

```
myPromise
  .then(result => {
    // Handle successful result
  })
  .catch(error => {
    // Handle error
  });
```

- **Promise Chaining:**
    - Promises can be chained together to perform a sequence of asynchronous operations.[7]
    - Each then() method returns a new Promise, allowing you to chain them.
    - **Example:**

JavaScript

```javascript
fetchData()
  .then(data => processData(data))
    .then(processedData    =>
displayData(processedData))
  .catch(error => handleError(error));
```

- **Promise.all():**
  - The Promise.all() method takes an array of Promises and returns a new Promise that fulfills when all of the input Promises fulfill.
  - It rejects as soon as one of the input Promises rejects.
  - **Example:**

JavaScript

```javascript
Promise.all([fetchData1(), fetchData2(),
fetchData3()])
  .then(results => {
  // All promises fulfilled
```

```
  console.log(results);
})
.catch(error => {
  // One or more promises rejected
  console.error(error);
});
```

- **Promise.race():**
    - The Promise.race() method takes an array of Promises and returns a new Promise that fulfills or rejects as soon as one of the input Promises fulfills or rejects.[8]
    - **Example:**

JavaScript

```
Promise.race([fetchData1(), fetchData2()])
  .then(result => {
    // First promise to resolve or reject
```

```
  console.log(result);
})
.catch(error => {
  console.error(error);
});
```

- **Advantages of Promises:**
  - **Readability:** Promises make asynchronous code more readable and easier to understand.[9]
  - **Error Handling:** Promises provide a centralized way to handle errors using catch().
  - **Chaining:** Promises allow you to chain asynchronous operations together in a clean and organized way.[10]
  - **Avoiding Callback Hell:** Promises eliminate the need for deeply nested callbacks.[11]

8.4. async and await: Simplifying Asynchronous Operations

- async **Functions:**
  - The async keyword is used to define asynchronous functions.
  - An async function always returns a Promise.
  - You can use the await keyword inside an async function to pause execution and wait for a Promise to resolve.
  - **Syntax:**

JavaScript

```javascript
async function myFunction() {
  // Asynchronous code here
}
```

- await **Keyword:**

- The await keyword is used to pause the execution of an async function until a Promise is resolved.
- It can only be used inside an async function.[12]
- **Syntax:**

JavaScript

```javascript
async function myFunction() {
  let result = await somePromise;
  // Code to be executed after the promise resolves
}
```

- **Example:**

JavaScript

```javascript
async function fetchDataAndDisplay() {
```

```
try {
  let data = await fetchData();
        let processedData = await
processData(data);
  displayData(processedData);
} catch (error) {
  handleError(error);
  }
}
```

- **Error Handling with** try...catch**:**
  - Errors in async/await functions are handled using try...catch blocks.
  - This makes error handling more straightforward and similar to synchronous code.
- **Advantages of** async/await**:**
  - **Readability:** async/await makes asynchronous code look and behave like synchronous code, improving readability and maintainability.

- Simplicity: It simplifies the syntax for handling asynchronous operations, making it easier to write and understand.
- **Error Handling:** try...catch blocks provide a familiar and effective way to handle errors.
- **Combining Promises and** async/await**:**
  - async/await is built on top of Promises. You can use Promises and async/await together in your code.
  - For example, you can use Promises to create asynchronous functions and then use async/await to consume those functions.

By mastering Promises and async/await, you can write clean, readable, and maintainable asynchronous code that handles time-consuming operations efficiently and effectively.

CHAPTER 9

Fetch API: Communicating with Servers

The Fetch API is a powerful and flexible tool that allows JavaScript to make network requests to servers. It provides a modern and standardized way to fetch resources, such as data, images, and HTML, from remote servers.

9.1. Making HTTP Requests: GET, POST, PUT, and DELETE

* **The Basics of HTTP Requests:**

* HTTP (Hypertext Transfer Protocol) is the foundation of data communication on the World Wide Web.

* HTTP requests are used to retrieve or send data between a client (e.g., a web browser) and a server.

* Different HTTP methods are used for different types of requests.

* **`fetch()` Function:**
    * The `fetch()` function is the core of the Fetch API. It returns a Promise that resolves to the `Response` object representing the server's response.
    * **Syntax:**

```javascript
fetch(url, options);
```

    * **`url`:** The URL of the resource to fetch.
    * **`options` (optional):** An object containing options for the request, such as the HTTP method, headers, and body.
* **HTTP Methods:**
    * **`GET`:**
        * Retrieves data from a server.
        * It's the most common HTTP method and is used for fetching resources.
        * **Example:**

```javascript
```

```javascript
fetch("https://api.example.com/data")
  .then(response => {
    // Handle response
  });
```

* **`POST`:**
    * Sends data to a server to create a new resource.
        * It's used for submitting forms, creating new records, or uploading files.
    * **Example:**

```javascript
fetch("https://api.example.com/data", {
  method: "POST",
  headers: {
    "Content-Type": "application/json"
  },
  body: JSON.stringify({ name: "John", age: 30 })
})
  .then(response => {
    // Handle response
```

```
    });
```
` ` `

* **`PUT`:**
    * Sends data to a server to update an existing resource.
        * It's used for modifying records or updating data.
    * **Example:**

```javascript
fetch("https://api.example.com/data/123", {
    method: "PUT",
    headers: {
      "Content-Type": "application/json"
    },
      body: JSON.stringify({ name: "Jane", age: 35 })
    })
    .then(response => {
      // Handle response
    });
```

```
```

* **`DELETE`:**
    * Sends a request to a server to delete a resource.
        * It's used for removing records or deleting data.
    * **Example:**

```javascript

fetch("https://api.example.com/data/123",
{
    method: "DELETE"
})
  .then(response => {
   // Handle response
  });
```

* **Headers:**
    * HTTP headers provide additional information about the request or response.

* They can be used to specify the content type, authentication credentials, or other metadata.
  * **Example:**

```javascript
fetch("https://api.example.com/data", {
  headers: {
    "Authorization": "Bearer token123"
  }
});
```

* **Body:**
  * The request body contains the data to be sent to the server.
    * It's used for `POST` and `PUT` requests.
    * The data is typically sent in JSON format.
  * **Example:**

```javascript
fetch("https://api.example.com/data", {
```

```javascript
  method: "POST",
    body: JSON.stringify({ name: "John",
age: 30 })
  });
```

9.2. Handling Responses: Parsing JSON Data

* **The `Response` Object:**
  * The `fetch()` function returns a Promise that resolves to a `Response` object.
    * The `Response` object contains information about the server's response, such as the status code, headers, and body.
* **Parsing JSON Data:**
  * The `json()` method of the `Response` object parses the response body as JSON and returns a Promise that resolves to the parsed data.
  * **Example:**

```javascript
fetch("https://api.example.com/data")
  .then(response => response.json())
```

```
  .then(data => {
   console.log(data);
  });
` ` `
```

* **Other Response Types:**
   * The `Response` object provides other methods for parsing different types of data:
      * **`text()`:** Parses the response body as plain text.
         * **`blob()`:** Parses the response body as a binary large object (BLOB).
            * **`arrayBuffer()`:** Parses the response body as an ArrayBuffer.
               * **`formData()`:** Parses the response body as FormData.

9.3. Working with API Endpoints

* **API Endpoints:**
   * API (Application Programming Interface) endpoints are URLs that provide access to specific resources or functionalities on a server.

* They are used to retrieve or send data to a server.
    * **Example:**
        * `https://api.example.com/users`
                                                    *
`https://api.example.com/products/123`
* **Using API Endpoints:**
    * You can use the `fetch()` function to make requests to API endpoints.
        * You can specify the HTTP method, headers, and body to interact with the API.
* **Authentication:**
        * Many APIs require authentication to access their resources.
            * Authentication can be done using headers, query parameters, or cookies.
    * **Example:**

```javascript
fetch("https://api.example.com/data", {
  headers: {
    "Authorization": "Bearer token123"
  }
});
```

```
```

9.4. Error Handling in Fetch Requests

* **Handling Network Errors:**
    * The `fetch()` function's Promise rejects only for network errors, not for HTTP errors (e.g., 404, 500).
    * You need to check the `ok` property of the `Response` object to determine if the request was successful.
    * **Example:**

```javascript
fetch("https://api.example.com/data")
  .then(response => {
    if (!response.ok) {
      throw new Error(`HTTP error! status: ${response.status}`);
    }
    return response.json();
  })
  .then(data => {
    console.log(data);
```

```javascript
})
.catch(error => {
  console.error("Fetch error:", error);
});
```

* **Handling JSON Parsing Errors:**
   * The `json()` method can throw an error if the response body is not valid JSON.
   * You should handle this error using a `try...catch` block.
   * **Example:**

```javascript
fetch("https://api.example.com/data")
  .then(response => response.text())
  .then(text => {
    try {
      const data = JSON.parse(text);
      console.log(data);
    } catch (error) {
        console.error("JSON parsing error:", error);
    }
```

```
})
.catch(error => {
  console.error("Fetch error:", error);
});
```
` ` `

* **Best Practices:**
    * Always check the `ok` property of the `Response` object.
    * Handle JSON parsing errors using `try...catch`.
    * Use descriptive error messages to help with debugging.
    * Consider using a library like `axios` or `superagent` for more advanced features and error handling.

By mastering the Fetch API, you can create dynamic and interactive web applications that communicate with servers and retrieve or send data effectively.

CHAPTER 10

Introduction to ES6+ Features: Modern JavaScript Practices

ES6 (ECMAScript 2015) and subsequent ECMAScript versions have brought a wealth of new features to JavaScript, making it more powerful, expressive, and developer-friendly.[1] These features have streamlined common tasks, improved code readability, and enabled more sophisticated programming patterns.[2]

10.1. Destructuring Assignment: Simplifying Data Extraction

- **The Problem of Tedious Data Extraction:**
  - Before ES6, extracting values from arrays or objects often

involved verbose and repetitive code.

- For example, accessing multiple properties of an object required multiple lines of code, making it cumbersome and less readable.

- **Destructuring to the Rescue:**
  - Destructuring assignment is a syntax that allows you to unpack values from arrays or properties from objects into distinct variables.[3]
  - It provides a concise and elegant way to extract data, improving code readability and reducing boilerplate.[4]

- **Array Destructuring:**
  - Array destructuring allows you to extract values from an array and assign them to variables.[5]
  - **Syntax:**

let [variable1, variable2, ...] = array;

* **Example:**

JavaScript

```
let numbers = [1, 2, 3, 4, 5];
let [first, second, , fourth] = numbers; // Skip the third element

console.log(first); // Output: 1
console.log(second); // Output: 2
console.log(fourth); // Output: 4
```

* **Default Values:**
    * You can assign default values to variables in case the corresponding array element is `undefined`.
    * **Example:**

JavaScript

```
let [a, b = 10] = [5];
console.log(a); // Output: 5
console.log(b); // Output: 10
```

* **Rest Parameter:**
    * You can use the rest parameter (`...`) to collect the remaining elements of an array into a new array.
    * **Example:**

JavaScript

```
let [x, y, ...rest] = [1, 2, 3, 4, 5];
console.log(rest); // Output: [3, 4, 5]
```

- **Object Destructuring:**
    - Object destructuring allows you to extract properties from an

object and assign them to variables.[67]

- ○ **Syntax:**

JavaScript

```
let { property1, property2, ... } = object;
```

* **Example:**

JavaScript

```
let person = { name: "John", age: 30, city: "New York" };
let { name, age } = person;

console.log(name); // Output: John
console.log(age); // Output: 30
```

* **Renaming Variables:**
    * You can rename variables during object destructuring using the colon syntax.
    * **Example:**

JavaScript

```
let { name: personName, age: personAge
} = person;
    console.log(personName); // Output:
John
    console.log(personAge); // Output: 30
```

* **Nested Object Destructuring:**
    * You can destructure nested objects to access properties within them.
    * **Example:**

JavaScript

```
let user = { profile: { firstName: "Jane",
lastName: "Doe" } };
    let { profile: { firstName } } = user;
    console.log(firstName); // Output: Jane
```

* **Default Values:**
    * You can assign default values to variables in case the corresponding object property is `undefined`.
    * **Example:**

JavaScript

```
let { city = "Unknown" } = person;
console.log(city); // Output: New York
```

- **Use Cases:**
    - Extracting values from arrays or objects returned by functions.[8]

- Swapping variables without using a temporary variable.[9]
- Passing configuration objects to functions.
- Simplifying data extraction from API responses.[10]

10.2. Spread and Rest Operators: Flexible Data Handling

- **The Power of ...:**
  - The spread and rest operators, both represented by ..., provide powerful ways to manipulate arrays and objects.
  - They allow you to expand or collect elements, making your code more flexible and expressive.[11]
- **Spread Operator (...):**

- The spread operator expands an iterable (e.g., array or string) into individual elements.[12]
- It can be used in array literals, object literals, and function calls.
- **Array Spread:**
  - Creating a new array by copying elements from an existing array.[13]
  - **Example:**

JavaScript

```
let numbers1 = [1, 2, 3];
let numbers2 = [...numbers1, 4, 5];
console.log(numbers2); // Output: [1, 2, 3, 4, 5]
```

* Concatenating arrays.
* **Example:**

JavaScript

```javascript
let combined = [...numbers1, ...numbers2];
console.log(combined); // Output: [1, 2, 3, 1, 2, 3, 4, 5]
```

* **Object Spread:**
    * Creating a new object by copying properties from an existing object.
    * **Example:**

JavaScript

```javascript
let person1 = { name: "John", age: 30 };
let person2 = { ...person1, city: "New York" };
console.log(person2); // Output: { name: "John", age: 30, city: "New York" }
```

* **Function Spread:**
    * Passing elements of an array as arguments to a function.
    * **Example:**

JavaScript

```
function sum(a, b, c) {
  return a + b + c;
}

let numbers = [1, 2, 3];
console.log(sum(...numbers)); // Output: 6
```

- **Rest Operator (...):**
    - The rest operator collects the remaining elements of an array or the remaining properties of an object into a new array or object.[14]

- It's used in function parameters and destructuring assignment.
- **Function Rest Parameter:**
  - Collecting multiple arguments into an array.
  - **Example:**
    -
- •

JavaScript

```javascript
function sum(...numbers) {
    return numbers.reduce((total, num) => total + num, 0);
}


    console.log(sum(1, 2, 3, 4, 5)); // Output: 15
```

* **Object Rest Parameter:**
    * Collecting the remaining properties of an object into a new object.

* **Example:**

JavaScript

```
let { name, ...details } = person1;
    console.log(details); // Output: { age:
30 }
```

- **Use Cases:**
  - Creating shallow copies of arrays and objects.
  - Merging arrays and objects.
  - Passing variable number of arguments to functions.
  - Collecting remaining elements or properties during destructuring.[15]

By mastering destructuring assignment and the spread/rest operators, you can write more concise, readable, and efficient JavaScript code.[16]

10.3. Template Literals: Enhancing String Interpolation

- **The Limitations of Traditional Strings:**
  - Before ES6, creating complex strings with embedded variables or multiline content was cumbersome and error-prone.
  - String concatenation using the + operator was verbose and difficult to read, especially when dealing with multiple variables.
  - Multiline strings required escaping newline characters or concatenating multiple string literals.[1]
- **Template Literals to the Rescue:**
  - Template literals, enclosed in backticks (`` ` ``), provide a more

elegant and expressive way to create strings.[2]

  o They allow you to embed variables directly within strings using string interpolation and to create multiline strings without escaping characters.[3]

- **String Interpolation:**
  o String interpolation allows you to embed variables or expressions directly within a string.[4]
  o It's done using the ${} syntax.
  o **Example:**

JavaScript

```
let name = "John";
let age = 30;
let message = `My name is ${name} and I am ${age} years old. `;
console.log(message); // Output: My name is John and I am 30 years old.
```

* **Expressions:**
    * You can embed any valid JavaScript expression within `${}`.
    * **Example:**

JavaScript

```
let a = 10;
let b = 20;
let result = `The sum of ${a} and ${b} is ${a + b}.`;
console.log(result); // Output: The sum of 10 and 20 is 30.
```

* **Function Calls:**
    * You can also embed function calls within `${}`.
    * **Example:**

JavaScript

```
function greet(name) {
  return `Hello, ${name}!`;
}

let greeting = `${greet("Alice")}`;
console.log(greeting); // Output: Hello, Alice!
```

- **Multiline Strings:**
  - Template literals allow you to create multiline strings without escaping newline characters.[5]
  - The backticks preserve the formatting of the string, including whitespace and newlines.[6]
  - **Example:**

JavaScript

```javascript
let multiline = `
  This is a
  multiline
  string.
  `;
console.log(multiline);
/* Output:
  This is a
  multiline
  string.
*/
```

- **Tagged Templates:**
    - Tagged templates are a more advanced feature that allows you to process template literals with a function.[7]
    - The function receives the template literal's raw string parts and the interpolated values as arguments.
    - **Example:**

JavaScript

```javascript
function highlight(strings, ...values) {
  let result = "";
  for (let i = 0; i < strings.length; i++) {
    result += strings[i];
    if (i < values.length) {
      result += `<span class="highlight">${values[i]}</span>`;
    }
  }
  return result;
}

let name = "John";
let age = 30;
let highlighted = highlight`My name is ${name} and I am ${age} years old.`;
console.log(highlighted);
// Output: My name is <span class="highlight">John</span> and I am <span class="highlight">30</span> years old.
```

- **Use Cases:**
  - Creating dynamic strings with embedded variables.
  - Generating HTML markup with interpolated values.
  - Creating multiline strings for better readability.
  - Implementing custom string processing with tagged templates.

10.4. Modules: Organizing Code for Reusability

- **The Problem of Global Scope:**
  - Before ES6 modules, JavaScript code was often organized using global variables and functions.
  - This led to naming collisions, code duplication, and difficulty in managing dependencies.

- Large codebases became increasingly difficult to maintain and understand.
- **Modules to the Rescue:**
  - ES6 modules provide a standardized way to organize JavaScript code into reusable units.[8]
  - Modules allow you to encapsulate code and expose only the necessary parts to other modules.[9]
  - This improves code maintainability, reduces naming collisions, and simplifies dependency management.
- **Exporting from Modules:**
  - The export keyword is used to make variables, functions, or classes available to other modules.
  - **Named Exports:**

- Exporting individual variables, functions, or classes.
- **Example:**

JavaScript

```
// module.js
export const PI = 3.14159;
export function add(a, b) {
  return a + b;
}
export class Circle {
  constructor(radius) {
    this.radius = radius;
  }
}
```

* **Default Exports:**
    * Exporting a single value as the default export of a module.

* **Example:**

JavaScript

```
// module.js
export default function greet(name) {
  return `Hello, ${name}!`;
}
```

- **Importing Modules:**
  - The import keyword is used to import variables, functions, or classes from other modules.
  - **Named Imports:**
    - Importing specific named exports from a module.
    - **Example:**

JavaScript

```
// main.js
    import { PI, add, Circle } from
"./module.js";
  console.log(PI);
  console.log(add(10, 20));
  let circle = new Circle(5);
```

* **Default Imports:**
    * Importing the default export from a module.
    * **Example:**

JavaScript

```
// main.js
import greet from "./module.js";
console.log(greet("Alice"));
```

* **Importing Everything:**
    * Importing all exports from a module into a namespace object.

* **Example:**

JavaScript

```
// main.js
        import * as MathUtils from
"./module.js";
   console.log(MathUtils.PI);
   console.log(MathUtils.add(10, 20));
```

- **Module Resolution:**
  - JavaScript uses a module resolution algorithm to determine the location of imported modules.[10]
  - Module resolution can be configured using module bundlers like Webpack or Rollup.[11]
- **Advantages of Modules:**

- Code Organization: Modules help organize code into logical units, improving maintainability.[12]
- Code Reusability: Modules promote code reusability by allowing you to share code across different parts of your application.[13]
- Dependency Management: Modules simplify dependency management by explicitly specifying module dependencies.
- Namespace Management: Modules create separate namespaces, preventing naming collisions.

By mastering template literals and modules, you can write more expressive, maintainable, and organized JavaScript code, enabling you to build complex and scalable applications.[14]

CHAPTER 11

Debugging and Error Handling: Writing Robust Code

Debugging and error handling are indispensable skills for any JavaScript developer. They allow you to identify and fix issues in your code, ensuring that your applications run smoothly and reliably.

11.1. Using the Browser Developer Tools for Debugging

- **The Power of Developer Tools:**
    - Modern browsers come equipped with powerful developer tools that provide a wealth of features for debugging JavaScript code.[1]
    - These tools allow you to inspect elements, set breakpoints, step

through code, and monitor network activity.[2]

- **Accessing Developer Tools:**
  - You can access developer tools by pressing F12 (or Cmd+Option+I on macOS) or by right-clicking on a web page and selecting "Inspect" or "Inspect Element."
- **Key Debugging Features:**
  - **Console:**
    - The console is used for logging messages, displaying errors, and executing JavaScript code.[3]
    - You can use console.log(), console.warn(), console.error(), and console.table() to output different types of messages.
    - The console also provides an interactive JavaScript

environment where you can execute code and inspect variables.[4]

- **Elements:**
  - The Elements tab allows you to inspect and modify the HTML and CSS of a web page.[5]
  - You can view the DOM tree, inspect element properties, and change styles in real-time.[6]
- **Sources (Debugger):**
  - The Sources tab is used for debugging JavaScript code.[7]
  - You can set breakpoints, step through code, inspect variables, and view the call stack.[8]
  - **Breakpoints:** Breakpoints pause the execution of your code at a specific line, allowing you

to inspect variables and step through the code.[9]

- **Step Over, Step Into, Step Out:** These buttons allow you to control the execution flow of your code.
- **Call Stack:** The call stack shows the sequence of function calls that led to the current point of execution.[10]

○ **Network:**

- The Network tab allows you to monitor network requests and responses.[11]
- You can inspect the headers, status codes, and content of requests and responses.[12]
- This is useful for debugging API calls and identifying network issues.

○ **Performance:**

- The Performance tab allows you to profile the performance of your web page.[13]
- You can record and analyze the execution time of different parts of your code.
- This is useful for identifying performance bottlenecks and optimizing your code.
  - **Application (Storage):**
    - The Application tab allows you to inspect and manage storage, like cookies, local storage, and session storage.[14]
- **Using Breakpoints Effectively:**
  - Set breakpoints at strategic locations in your code, such as function calls, loops, or conditional statements.

- Use conditional breakpoints to pause execution only when a specific condition is met.
- Inspect the values of variables and the call stack to understand the state of your application.

- **Debugging Techniques:**
  - **Rubber Duck Debugging:** Explain your code to an inanimate object (like a rubber duck) to identify errors in your logic.
  - **Divide and Conquer:** Break down your code into smaller parts and test each part individually.[15]
  - **Logging:** Use console.log() statements to log the values of variables and the execution flow of your code.
  - **Binary Search Debugging:** If you have a large block of code, comment out half of it and see if the error still occurs. Repeat this

process to narrow down the source of the error.

11.2. Identifying and Fixing Common Errors

- **Syntax Errors:**
  - Syntax errors occur when your code violates the rules of the JavaScript language.[16]
  - Examples: missing semicolons, mismatched brackets, or incorrect keywords.
  - The browser console will typically display a syntax error message with the line number and a description of the error.
- **Reference Errors:**
  - Reference errors occur when you try to access a variable or function that is not defined.[17]

- Examples: using an undeclared variable or calling a function that doesn't exist.
- The browser console will display a reference error message with the name of the undefined variable or function.
- **Type Errors:**
  - Type errors occur when you try to perform an operation on a value of an incorrect type.[18]
  - Examples: calling a method on an undefined object or trying to add a number to a string.
  - The browser console will display a type error message with the type of the error.[19]
- **Logical Errors:**
  - Logical errors occur when your code runs without throwing an error, but it doesn't produce the expected result.[20]

- Examples: incorrect calculations, wrong conditional statements, or infinite loops.
- Logical errors are often the most difficult to find and fix.
- **Debugging Strategies:**
  - **Read Error Messages Carefully:** Error messages often provide valuable clues about the source of the problem.
  - **Use the Debugger:** Set breakpoints and step through your code to inspect variables and the execution flow.
  - **Test Your Code Thoroughly:** Write unit tests to verify the correctness of your code.
  - **Use a Linter:** Linters can help you identify potential errors and enforce coding standards.[21]

11.3. Try-Catch Blocks: Handling Exceptions

- **The Need for Exception Handling:**
  - Exceptions are runtime errors that can occur during the execution of your code.[22]
  - They can be caused by various factors, such as invalid input, network errors, or unexpected conditions.[23]
  - Exception handling allows you to gracefully handle these errors and prevent your application from crashing.[24]
- try...catch **Blocks:**
  - try...catch blocks are used to handle exceptions in JavaScript.
  - The try block contains the code that might throw an exception.

- The catch block contains the code that is executed if an exception occurs.
- **Syntax:**

JavaScript

```javascript
try {
  // Code that might throw an exception
} catch (error) {
  // Code to handle the exception
} finally {
  // code to be executed regardless of if an error occurred.
}
```

* **Example:**

JavaScript

```
try {
    let result = 10 / 0; // This will throw an
exception
    console.log(result);
  } catch (error) {
        console.error("An error occurred:",
error);
  }
```

- finally **Block:**
    - o The finally block is optional and contains code that is executed regardless of whether an exception occurred.
    - o It's often used for cleanup tasks, such as closing files or releasing resources.
- **Throwing Exceptions:**
    - o You can manually throw exceptions using the throw keyword.
    - o This is useful for signaling errors in your own code.

○ **Example:**

JavaScript

```
function divide(a, b) {
  if (b === 0) {
    throw new Error("Division by zero is
not allowed.");
  }
  return a / b;
}
```

11.4. Best Practices for Debugging and Error Prevention

- **Write Clean and Readable Code:**
  - ○ Clear and well-structured code is easier to debug and maintain.
- **Use Meaningful Variable and Function Names:**

- o Descriptive names make your code more self-documenting.
- **Test Your Code Regularly:**
  - o Write unit tests and integration tests to verify the correctness of your code.
- **Use a Linter:**
  - o Linters can help you identify potential errors and enforce coding standards.[25]
- **Handle Errors Gracefully:**
  - o Use try...catch blocks to handle exceptions and prevent your application from crashing.
- **Log Errors and Exceptions:**
  - o Log error messages and stack traces to help with debugging.
- **Use Version Control:**
  - o Version control systems like Git allow you to track changes to your code and revert to previous versions if needed.[26]
- **Code Reviews:**

- Have your code reviewed by other developers to identify potential errors and improve code quality.
- **Early Returns:**
  - Use early returns to simplify conditional logic and reduce nesting.
- **Defensive Programming:**
  - Anticipate potential errors and write code that handles them gracefully.
- **Embrace a Debugging Mindset:**
  - View debugging as a learning opportunity and a chance to improve your code.

By following these best practices, you can write robust and reliable JavaScript code that is easier to debug and maintain.

CHAPTER 12

Introduction to JavaScript Libraries and Frameworks

JavaScript libraries and frameworks are collections of pre-written code that provide developers with reusable components and functionalities.[1] They streamline development, reduce boilerplate code, and enable the creation of complex applications more efficiently.[2]

12.1. Understanding the Role of Libraries and Frameworks

- **Libraries: Tools for Specific Tasks:**
  - Libraries are collections of functions and objects that provide specific functionalities,

such as DOM manipulation, data processing, or animation.

- They are typically focused on solving a particular problem or set of problems.
- Libraries are integrated into your code as needed, providing modular and reusable components.[3]
- They offer a set of tools that you can use as building blocks for your application.

- **Frameworks: Architectural Structures:**
  - Frameworks provide a complete architectural structure for building applications.[4]
  - They define the overall structure, flow, and conventions of your application.[5]
  - Frameworks often include libraries and tools for various tasks, such as routing, state

management, and component rendering.[6]
- They offer a pre-defined way of doing things, providing a consistent and structured approach to development.[7]

- **Key Differences:**
  - **Control:** Libraries give you control over how and when to use their functionalities, while frameworks impose a specific structure and flow.
  - **Scope:** Libraries are typically focused on specific tasks, while frameworks provide a comprehensive solution for building entire applications.
  - **Inversion of Control:** Frameworks often use inversion of control (IoC), where the framework calls your code, while libraries are called by your code.[8]

- **Benefits:**

- **Increased Productivity:** Libraries and frameworks reduce development time by providing pre-built components and functionalities.[9]
- **Code Reusability:** They promote code reusability, reducing duplication and improving maintainability.[10]
- **Improved Performance:** Many libraries and frameworks are optimized for performance, leading to faster and more efficient applications.[11]
- **Community Support:** Popular libraries and frameworks have large communities, providing extensive documentation, tutorials, and support.[12]
- **Consistency:** Frameworks enforce a consistent coding style and structure, making it easier for teams to collaborate.[13]

12.2. An Overview of Popular Libraries: jQuery, Lodash, etc.

- **jQuery:**
  - A fast, small, and feature-rich JavaScript library.
  - Simplifies HTML document traversal and manipulation, event handling,[14] animation, and Ajax.[15]
  - Provides a cross-browser compatible way to interact with the DOM.
  - **Use Cases:** DOM manipulation, event handling, animations, Ajax requests.
  - **Example:**

JavaScript

```
// Select all paragraphs and add a class
$("p").addClass("highlight");
```

```
// Handle click event on a button
$("#myButton").click(function() {
  alert("Button clicked!");
});
```

- **Lodash:**
  - ○ A modern JavaScript utility library delivering modularity, performance, and extras.[16]
  - ○ Provides a wide range of functions for array manipulation, object manipulation, function manipulation, and more.
  - ○ Offers consistent cross-environment iteration support for arrays, objects, and strings.
  - ○ **Use Cases:** Data manipulation, functional programming, utility functions.
  - ○ **Example:**

JavaScript

```javascript
// Deep clone an object
let clonedObject = _.cloneDeep(myObject);

// Group an array of objects by a property
let groupedData = _.groupBy(myData, "category");
```

- **Moment.js (Deprecated, but historically important):**
  - A JavaScript library for parsing, validating, manipulating, and formatting dates.[17]
  - Provides a simple and intuitive API for working with dates and times.
  - **Use Cases:** Date and time manipulation, formatting, parsing.

- **Replacement:** Libraries like Date-fns and Luxon are now recommended.
- **Axios:**
  - A promise-based HTTP client for the browser and Node.js.[18]
  - Provides a simple and intuitive API for making HTTP requests.
  - Offers features like interceptors, automatic JSON transformation, and client-side support for protecting against XSRF.
  - **Use Cases:** Making HTTP requests to APIs, handling responses.

12.3. Introduction to Modern Frameworks: React, Vue, Angular

- **React:**

- A JavaScript library for building user interfaces.
- Developed and maintained by Facebook.
- Uses a component-based architecture, where UI elements are broken down into reusable components.[19]
- Employs a virtual DOM for efficient updates.[20]
- **Key Concepts:** Components, JSX, state, props, hooks.
- **Use Cases:** Building complex UIs, single-page applications (SPAs), mobile apps (React Native).

- **Vue.js:**
  - A progressive JavaScript framework for building user interfaces.[21]
  - Known for its simplicity and ease of learning.

- Uses a component-based architecture and a reactive data binding system.[22]
- Provides a gentle learning curve and excellent documentation.
- **Key Concepts:** Components, templates, data binding, directives, computed properties.
- **Use Cases:** Building interactive UIs, SPAs, progressive web apps (PWAs).

- **Angular:**
  - A platform and framework for building single-page client applications using HTML and TypeScript.[23]
  - Developed and maintained by Google.[24]
  - Provides a comprehensive set of tools and features, including routing, dependency injection, and form handling.[25]
  - Uses a component-based architecture and a powerful CLI.

- Key Concepts: Components, modules, services, directives, dependency injection.
- Use Cases: Building large-scale enterprise applications, complex SPAs.[26]

12.4. Choosing the Right Tools for Your Project

- **Project Requirements:**
  - Consider the complexity, scale, and specific requirements of your project.
  - For simple projects, a library might be sufficient.
  - For complex projects, a framework might be necessary.
- **Team Expertise:**
  - Choose tools that your team is familiar with or can learn quickly.

- Consider the learning curve and the availability of resources.
- **Performance Considerations:**
  - Evaluate the performance characteristics of different libraries and frameworks.
  - Choose tools that are optimized for your specific use case.
- **Community and Support:**
  - Consider the size and activity of the community around a library or framework.
  - Choose tools with good documentation, tutorials, and support.
- **Future Maintainability:**
  - Select tools that are actively maintained and have a clear roadmap for future development.
- **Project Size:**
  - For small projects, jQuery or Lodash could be sufficient.

- For medium to large projects, React, Vue, or Angular are recommended.
- **Learning Curve:**
  - Vue.js has a gentle learning curve, while Angular has a steeper learning curve.[27] React is in the middle.
- **Personal Preference:**
  - Ultimately, the best tool for your project depends on your personal preferences and your team's experience.

By understanding the roles of libraries and frameworks and carefully evaluating your project requirements, you can choose the right tools to build efficient and maintainable JavaScript applications.

CHAPTER 13

Building a Simple Web Application: Putting It All Together

This chapter serves as a culmination of all the knowledge acquired, guiding you through the process of developing a functional web application from planning to deployment. We'll focus on a practical example, such as a simple to-do list application, to illustrate the process.

13.1. Project Planning and Design

- Defining the Application's Purpose:
    - Clearly define the application's purpose and functionality.
    - What problem does it solve? What features will it have?

- For our to-do list application, the purpose is to provide a simple way to manage and track tasks.
- User Stories and Requirements:
  - Create user stories to outline the application's features from the user's perspective.
  - Example: "As a user, I want to add a task to my to-do list."
  - Define functional and non-functional requirements.
  - Functional: Adding tasks, marking tasks as complete, deleting tasks.
  - Non-functional: Performance, usability, security.[1]
- Wireframing and UI Design:
  - Create wireframes to visualize the layout and structure of the application's user interface.[2]
  - Use tools like Figma, Balsamiq, or even pen and paper.[3]

- Design the UI with a focus on simplicity and usability.
- Consider the user experience (UX) and ensure that the application is intuitive to use.
- Technology Stack Selection:
  - Choose the technologies that will be used to build the application.
  - For our to-do list app, we'll use:
    - HTML for structure
    - CSS for styling
    - JavaScript for functionality
    - (Optional) Local Storage for data persistence.
- Project Structure:
  - Organize your project files into a logical structure.
  - Example:
    - index.html
    - styles.css
    - script.js
    - (Optional) assets/ (for images, icons, etc.)

13.2. Implementing Functionality with JavaScript

- DOM Manipulation:
  - Use JavaScript to manipulate the DOM and create the dynamic elements of the application.[4]
  - Create functions to add, remove, and update tasks in the to-do list.
  - Example:

JavaScript

```
function addTask(taskText) {
    let taskItem = document.createElement("li");
    taskItem.textContent = taskText;

document.getElementById("taskList").appendChild(taskItem);
```

}

- Event Handling:
  - Use event listeners to respond to user interactions, such as clicking buttons or submitting forms.[5]
  - Implement event handlers for adding tasks, marking tasks as complete, and deleting tasks.
  - Example:

JavaScript

```
document.getElementById("addButton").ad
dEventListener("click", function() {
            let taskInput =
document.getElementById("taskInput");
   addTask(taskInput.value);
   taskInput.value = "";
```

```
});
```

- Data Management:
  - Decide how you will store and manage the application's data.
  - For a simple to-do list, you can use an array to store the tasks in memory.
  - (Optional) Use local storage to persist the data between browser sessions.[6]
  - Example:

JavaScript

```
let tasks = [];

function addTask(taskText) {
    tasks.push({ text: taskText, completed:
false });
    // ... update DOM ...
```

```
        }

        // (Optional) Local Storage
        function saveTasks() {
                localStorage.setItem("tasks",
        JSON.stringify(tasks));
        }

        function loadTasks() {
                let    storedTasks    =
        localStorage.getItem("tasks");
          if (storedTasks) {
            tasks = JSON.parse(storedTasks);
            // ... update DOM ...
          }
        }
```

- Modularization:
    - Break down your JavaScript code into smaller, reusable functions.

- Use modules (if applicable) to organize your code and manage dependencies.[7]

13.3. Styling with CSS and Structuring with HTML

- HTML Structure:
  - Create the HTML structure of the application using semantic HTML elements.
  - Use elements like div, ul, li, input, and button to create the layout of the to-do list.
  - Example:

HTML

```
<!DOCTYPE html>
<html>
```

```html
<head>
  <title>To-Do List</title>
  <link rel="stylesheet" href="styles.css">
</head>
<body>
  <div id="app">
    <h1>To-Do List</h1>
        <input type="text" id="taskInput" placeholder="Enter task...">
                                <button id="addButton">Add</button>
    <ul id="taskList"></ul>
  </div>
  <script src="script.js"></script>
</body>
</html>
```

- CSS Styling:
    - Use CSS to style the application's user interface.
    - Create a visually appealing and user-friendly design.

- Use CSS selectors to target specific elements and apply styles.
- Example:

CSS

```
body {
  font-family: sans-serif;
  margin: 20px;
}

#app {
  width: 400px;
  margin: 0 auto;
}

#taskList li {
  padding: 10px;
  border-bottom: 1px solid #ccc;
}
```

- Responsive Design (Optional):
    - If desired, implement responsive design to ensure that the application looks good on different screen sizes.
    - Use media queries to apply different styles based on screen width.

13.4. Deployment and Testing

- Testing:
    - Test the application thoroughly to ensure that it functions correctly.
    - Test all features and edge cases.
    - Use the browser developer tools to debug any issues.
    - Test on different browsers and devices.
- Deployment:

- Choose a hosting platform to deploy your application.
- Options include:
  - GitHub Pages (for static websites)[8]
  - Netlify
  - Vercel
  - AWS S3
  - Firebase Hosting
- Follow the deployment instructions for your chosen platform.
- For GitHub pages, you simply need to create a repository, add your files, and enable GitHub pages in the repository settings.
- Continuous Integration/Continuous Deployment (CI/CD) (Optional):
  - Set up a CI/CD pipeline to automate the testing and deployment process.
  - Tools like GitHub Actions, GitLab CI/CD, or Jenkins can be used.

- Maintenance and Updates:
  - After deployment, monitor the application for errors and performance issues.
  - Plan for future updates and enhancements.
  - Gather user feedback to improve the application.

By following these steps, you can successfully build and deploy a simple web application, gaining valuable experience in the process. Remember to iterate and refine your application based on user feedback and your own observations.

CHAPTER 14

JavaScript in Non-Browser Environments: Node.js Basics

Node.js has revolutionized JavaScript development by enabling developers to use the same language for both client-side and server-side programming.[1] This chapter will introduce you to the fundamentals of Node.js and how to create server-side applications.

14.1. Introduction to Node.js and Server-Side JavaScript

- **The Evolution of JavaScript:**
  - Historically, JavaScript was primarily used for client-side scripting in web browsers.[2]
  - Node.js, built on the V8 JavaScript engine (used in Chrome), allows JavaScript to

run outside of the browser, enabling server-side development.[3]

- **What is Node.js?**
  - Node.js is a runtime environment that executes JavaScript code outside of a web browser.[4]
  - It's event-driven, non-blocking, and uses a single-threaded, asynchronous model, making it highly efficient for I/O-intensive applications.[5]
  - Node.js is designed to build scalable network applications, such as web servers, APIs, and real-time applications.[6]
- **Server-Side JavaScript:**
  - Server-side JavaScript allows you to use JavaScript to build the backend of web applications, including:
    - Handling HTTP requests and responses.

- Interacting with databases.
- Managing file systems.
- Building APIs.
- Creating real-time applications using WebSockets.

- **Key Features of Node.js:**
  - **Event-Driven, Non-Blocking I/O:** Node.js uses an event loop to handle asynchronous operations, allowing it to efficiently handle a large number of concurrent connections.[7]
  - **Single-Threaded:** Node.js uses a single thread to execute JavaScript code, which simplifies programming and reduces overhead.[8]
  - **NPM (Node Package Manager):** NPM is a package manager that allows you to easily install and manage

third-party libraries and modules.[9]

- **Cross-Platform:** Node.js runs on various operating systems, including Windows, macOS, and Linux.
- **Large Ecosystem:** Node.js has a vast ecosystem of modules and frameworks that provide a wide range of functionalities.[10]

- **Use Cases for Node.js:**
  - **Web Servers:** Building high-performance web servers and APIs.
  - **Real-Time Applications:** Creating chat applications, online games, and other real-time applications.
  - **Command-Line Tools:** Building command-line tools for automation and scripting.
  - **Data Streaming:** Processing and manipulating data streams.

- ○ **Microservices:** Building microservices architectures.
- ○ **Desktop Applications:** Building cross-platform desktop applications using frameworks like Electron.[11]

14.2. Setting Up Node.js and Running Scripts

- **Installing Node.js:**
  - ○ Download the Node.js installer from the official Node.js website (nodejs.org).[12]
  - ○ Choose the appropriate installer for your operating system.
  - ○ Follow the installation instructions.
  - ○ Verify the installation by running node -v and npm -v in your terminal.
- **Running JavaScript Scripts:**

- Create a JavaScript file (e.g., script.js).
- Write your JavaScript code in the file.
- Run the script using the node command in your terminal: node script.js.
- **Example:**

JavaScript

```
// script.js
console.log("Hello, Node.js!");
```

* Run: `node script.js`
* Output: `Hello, Node.js!`

- **REPL (Read-Eval-Print Loop):**
  - Node.js provides an interactive REPL environment where you

can execute JavaScript code directly in the terminal.[13]

- Start the REPL by running node in your terminal.
- Type JavaScript code and press Enter to execute it.
- Use .exit or Ctrl+C to exit the REPL.

14.3. Using npm for Package Management

- **What is npm?**
  - npm (Node Package Manager) is a package manager for JavaScript.[14]
  - It allows you to easily install, manage, and share JavaScript packages (libraries and modules).

- npm is bundled with Node.js, so you don't need to install it separately.[15]
- package.json:
  - The package.json file is a manifest file that contains metadata about your project and its dependencies.
  - It's used to manage project dependencies, scripts, and other settings.
  - Create a package.json file by running npm init in your project directory.
  - Follow the prompts to configure your project.
- **Installing Packages:**
  - Use the npm install command to install packages.
  - **Example:** npm install express
  - Packages are installed in the node_modules directory.

- Add the --save flag to add the package to your package.json dependencies.
- Add the --save-dev flag to add the package to your package.json devDependencies (for development tools).
- **Using Packages:**
  - Import packages into your JavaScript code using the require() function.
  - **Example:**

JavaScript

```
// server.js
const express = require("express");
const app = express();
// ...
```

- **Running Scripts from package.json:**
  - You can define scripts in the package.json file's scripts section.
  - Run scripts using the npm run command.
  - **Example:**

JSON

```json
{
  "scripts": {
    "start": "node server.js",
    "dev": "nodemon server.js"
  }
}
```

* Run: `npm run start` or `npm run dev`

14.4. Basic Server Creation with Node.js

- **Using the** http **Module:**
  - ○ The http module is a built-in Node.js module that allows you to create HTTP servers.
  - ○ **Example:**

JavaScript

```javascript
const http = require("http");

const server = http.createServer((req, res) => {
    res.writeHead(200, { "Content-Type": "text/plain" });
    res.end("Hello, Node.js Server!");
});

const port = 3000;
server.listen(port, () => {
```

```javascript
    console.log(`Server running on port
${port}`);
  });
```

- **Using Express.js:**
  - Express.js is a popular web framework for Node.js that simplifies the process of creating web servers and APIs.[16]
  - Install Express.js using npm install express.
  - **Example:**

JavaScript

```javascript
const express = require("express");
const app = express();

app.get("/", (req, res) => {
  res.send("Hello, Express.js!");
});
```

```javascript
const port = 3000;
app.listen(port, () => {
    console.log(`Server running on port ${port}`);
});
```

- **Routing:**
    - Routing is the process of defining how the server responds to different HTTP requests.[17]
    - Express.js provides a simple and intuitive way to define routes.[18]
    - **Example:**

JavaScript

```javascript
app.get("/users", (req, res) => {
    res.json([{ name: "Alice" }, { name: "Bob" }]);
```

```
});
```

- **Middleware:**
  - Middleware functions are functions that have access to the request object (req), the response object (res), and the[19] next middleware function in the application's request-response cycle.[20]
  - They can perform various tasks, such as logging, authentication, and error handling.
  - **Example:**

JavaScript

```
app.use((req, res, next) => {
    console.log(`Request: ${req.method}
${req.url}`);
    next();
```

```
});
```

By mastering these Node.js basics, you can build powerful and scalable server-side applications using JavaScript. Remember to explore the vast ecosystem of npm packages and frameworks to further enhance your development capabilities.

CHAPTER 15

Best Practices and Further Learning: Becoming a Proficient JavaScript Developer

Becoming a proficient JavaScript developer is an ongoing journey that requires continuous learning, practice, and a commitment to best practices. This chapter will provide you with guidance on how to refine your skills and stay ahead in the ever-evolving world of JavaScript.

15.1. Code Style and Readability

- **The Importance of Clean Code:**
  - Clean, readable code is essential for maintainability, collaboration, and debugging.
  - It makes your code easier to understand, modify, and extend.

- Consistent code style improves collaboration and reduces the cognitive load on developers.
- **Coding Style Guides:**
  - Follow established coding style guides, such as:
    - **Airbnb JavaScript Style Guide:** A widely adopted and comprehensive style guide.
    - **Google JavaScript Style Guide:** Another popular and well-maintained style guide.
    - **StandardJS:** A style guide with automatic code formatting.
  - These guides provide rules for indentation, naming conventions, variable declaration, and other aspects of code style.
- **Key Principles:**

- **Consistent Indentation:** Use consistent indentation (e.g., 2 or 4 spaces) to improve code readability.
- **Meaningful Variable and Function Names:** Choose descriptive names that clearly indicate the purpose of variables and functions.
- **Comments and Documentation:** Add comments to explain complex logic or non-obvious code. Use JSDoc or similar tools to generate documentation.
- **Avoid Magic Numbers:** Use named constants instead of hardcoded numbers.
- **Keep Functions Short and Focused:** Each function should have a single, well-defined responsibility.
- **Use Consistent Naming Conventions:** Follow a

consistent naming convention for variables, functions, and classes (e.g., camelCase, PascalCase).

- ○ **Write Modular Code:** Break down your code into smaller, reusable modules or components.
- ○ **Use Linters:** Linters like ESLint can automatically detect and fix code style issues.
- **Code Formatting Tools:**
  - ○ Use code formatters like Prettier to automatically format your code according to a style guide.
  - ○ This ensures consistency and reduces the effort of manually formatting code.
- **Code Reviews:**
  - ○ Participate in code reviews to receive feedback on your code style and identify areas for improvement.

- Provide constructive feedback to others and learn from their insights.

15.2. Performance Optimization Techniques

- **The Importance of Performance:**
  - Performance is crucial for providing a smooth and responsive user experience.
  - Slow-performing applications can lead to user frustration and abandonment.
  - Optimizing performance improves the efficiency and scalability of your applications.
- **Performance Optimization Strategies:**
  - **Minimize HTTP Requests:** Reduce the number of HTTP requests by combining and

minifying CSS and JavaScript files.

- **Use a Content Delivery Network (CDN):** Serve static assets (images, CSS, JavaScript) from a CDN to improve loading times.
- **Optimize Images:** Compress and resize images to reduce their file size.
- **Use Caching:** Implement caching strategies to store frequently accessed data and reduce server load.
- **Optimize JavaScript Code:**
  - **Avoid Global Variables:** Minimize the use of global variables to prevent naming collisions and improve performance.
  - **Use Efficient Data Structures:** Choose appropriate data

structures for your needs (e.g., Maps, Sets).

- **Minimize DOM Manipulation:** Batch DOM updates and avoid unnecessary reflows and repaints.

- **Use Event Delegation:** Attach event listeners to parent elements instead of individual child elements.

- **Optimize Loops:** Use efficient loop constructs and minimize operations within loops.

- **Use Web Workers:** Offload computationally intensive tasks to Web Workers to prevent blocking the main thread.

- **Use requestAnimationFrame:** Use requestAnimationFrame()

for animations to ensure smooth rendering.

- **Profile Your Code:** Use browser developer tools or profiling tools to identify performance bottlenecks.

- **Lazy Loading:** Load resources (images, scripts) only when they are needed.

- **Code Splitting:** Break down your code into smaller chunks that can be loaded on demand.

- **Use Performance Monitoring Tools:** Tools such as Google PageSpeed Insights, Lighthouse, and WebPageTest can help you analyze and improve your website's performance.

15.3. Staying Up-to-Date with JavaScript Trends

- **The Ever-Evolving JavaScript Ecosystem:**
  - JavaScript is a rapidly evolving language, with new features, libraries, and frameworks being released regularly.
  - Staying up-to-date with these trends is essential for maintaining your skills and building modern applications.
- **Strategies for Staying Current:**
  - **Follow JavaScript Blogs and Websites:**
    - Read articles and tutorials on popular JavaScript blogs and websites (e.g., MDN Web Docs, CSS-Tricks, Smashing Magazine).
  - **Subscribe to Newsletters:**

- Subscribe to newsletters that provide updates on JavaScript news and trends.
  - **Attend Conferences and Meetups:**
    - Attend JavaScript conferences and meetups to learn from experts and network with other developers.
  - **Follow JavaScript Influencers on Social Media:**
    - Follow JavaScript experts and influencers on Twitter, GitHub, and other social media platforms.
  - **Contribute to Open Source Projects:**
    - Contributing to open source projects allows you to learn from experienced developers and stay

up-to-date with best practices.

- **Experiment with New Technologies:**
  - Try out new JavaScript libraries, frameworks, and tools to expand your knowledge and skills.
- **Read the ECMAScript Specification:**
  - Stay informed about the latest ECMAScript proposals and features.
- **Take Online Courses and Tutorials:**
  - Enroll in online courses and tutorials to learn new JavaScript concepts and techniques.

15.4. Resources for Continued Learning

- **Documentation:**
  - **MDN Web Docs:** A comprehensive resource for web development technologies, including JavaScript.
  - **ECMAScript Specification:** The official specification for the JavaScript language.
- **Online Courses and Tutorials:**
  - **freeCodeCamp:** A free, open-source platform that offers coding challenges and projects.
  - **Codecademy:** Offers interactive courses on JavaScript and other programming languages.
  - **Udemy:** Provides a wide range of paid and free courses on JavaScript and web development.

- **Coursera:** Offers courses and specializations from top universities and institutions.
- **Frontend Masters:** Provides in-depth courses on front-end development.

- **Books:**
  - **"You Don't Know JS" series by Kyle Simpson:** A deep dive into the core concepts of JavaScript.
  - **"Eloquent JavaScript" by Marijn Haverbeke:** A comprehensive introduction to JavaScript programming.
  - **"JavaScript: The Definitive Guide" by David Flanagan:** A comprehensive reference for JavaScript.
  - **"Effective JavaScript" by David Herman:** A guide to writing high-quality JavaScript code.

- **Community Resources:**

- **Stack Overflow:** A question-and-answer site for programming-related questions.
- **GitHub:** A platform for hosting and collaborating on open-source projects.
- **Reddit (r/javascript, r/learnjavascript):** Online communities for JavaScript developers.
- **Discord and Slack Communities:** Join online communities for real-time discussions and support.
- **Blogs and Websites:**
  - **CSS-Tricks:** A website dedicated to front-end development.
  - **Smashing Magazine:** A website with articles and tutorials on web design and development.

- JavaScript Weekly: A weekly newsletter with JavaScript news and articles.
- Dev.to: A platform for sharing programming knowledge and experiences.

By embracing continuous learning and following these best practices, you can become a proficient JavaScript developer and build exceptional web applications. Remember that the journey of learning is as important as the destination.

Conclusion: Your JavaScript Journey Begins

This comprehensive guide has taken you through the foundational and advanced concepts of JavaScript, equipping you with the knowledge and skills to embark on your journey as a proficient developer. We've covered a vast landscape, from the basics of variables and functions to the complexities of asynchronous programming and server-side development. Now, let's consolidate what we've learned and look ahead.

Recap of Key Concepts and Skills

- **Fundamentals:**
    - We started with the foundational building blocks: variables, data types, operators, and control flow.
    - We explored functions, the core of modular and reusable code, including function scope, closures, and arrow functions.
- **Data Structures:**
    - We delved into arrays and objects, mastering their manipulation and iteration.
    - We learned how to represent real-world entities using objects

and how to exchange data using JSON.[1]

- **DOM Manipulation and Events:**
  - We conquered the Document Object Model (DOM), learning to interact with web pages dynamically.
  - We mastered event handling, enabling us to create interactive and responsive user experiences.
- **Asynchronous JavaScript:**
  - We navigated the complexities of asynchronous programming, understanding callbacks, promises, and async/await.
  - We learned to handle time-consuming operations without blocking the main thread.[2]
- **Server-Side JavaScript with Node.js:**
  - We ventured into the world of Node.js, learning to run JavaScript outside the browser.[3]

- We explored npm, created basic servers, and understood the potential of server-side JavaScript.
- **Modern JavaScript (ES6+):**
  - We embraced the power of ES6+ features, including destructuring, spread/rest operators, template literals, and modules.[4]
  - We explored the fetch API, and how to communicate with servers.
- **Debugging and Error Handling:**
  - We learned to use browser developer tools, identify and fix common errors, and handle exceptions with try...catch blocks.
- **Libraries and Frameworks:**
  - We gained an overview of popular libraries like jQuery and Lodash, and modern

frameworks like React, Vue, and Angular.

- **Best Practices:**
  - We emphasized the importance of code style, readability, performance optimization, and continuous learning.

Encouragement for Further Exploration

- **Practice, Practice, Practice:**
  - The best way to solidify your knowledge is through consistent practice.
  - Build personal projects, contribute to open-source, and solve coding challenges.
- **Dive Deeper into Frameworks:**
  - Choose a framework (React, Vue, or Angular) and explore its intricacies.

- Build complex applications and master its ecosystem.
- **Explore Advanced Topics:**
  - Delve into advanced JavaScript concepts, such as:
    - WebSockets for real-time communication.[5]
    - Web Workers for background processing.
    - Service Workers for offline capabilities.
    - Typescript, for adding static typing to your javascript.[6]
    - Web assembly, for running other languages inside of the browser.[7]
- **Build a Portfolio:**
  - Create a portfolio of your projects to showcase your skills to potential employers.
  - Contribute to open-source projects to demonstrate your collaboration skills.

- **Join the Community:**
  - Engage with the JavaScript community through forums, meetups, and online groups.
  - Network with other developers and learn from their experiences.
- **Never Stop Learning:**
  - The JavaScript landscape is constantly evolving.
  - Embrace continuous learning and stay curious.

The Future of JavaScript and Its Impact

- **JavaScript's Ubiquity:**
  - JavaScript's versatility has made it the language of the web, and its reach continues to expand.

- It's used in front-end, back-end, mobile, desktop, and even IoT development.
- **WebAssembly and Interoperability:**
  - WebAssembly (Wasm) allows other languages to run in the browser, expanding the capabilities of web applications.[8]
  - JavaScript will continue to play a crucial role in orchestrating and interacting with Wasm modules.
- **Serverless Computing:**
  - Node.js is a key player in the serverless computing revolution, enabling developers to build scalable and cost-effective applications.[9]
- **AI and Machine Learning:**
  - JavaScript is increasingly being used in AI and machine learning applications, particularly in browser-based models.[10]

- Libraries like TensorFlow.js bring machine learning capabilities to the front-end.[11]
- **Progressive Web Apps (PWAs):**
  - PWAs are blurring the lines between web and native applications, providing enhanced user experiences.[12]
  - JavaScript is the foundation of PWAs, enabling features like offline access and push notifications.
- **The Continued Evolution of ECMAScript:**
  - The ECMAScript standard continues to evolve, bringing new features and improvements to the language.[13]
  - Stay informed about the latest proposals and features to leverage the full potential of JavaScript.
- **JavaScript's Impact:**

- JavaScript has a profound impact on the way we interact with technology.
- It powers the dynamic web experiences we enjoy every day.
- It enables developers to build innovative applications that solve real-world problems.
- It democratizes web development, making it accessible to a wider audience.

Your JavaScript journey has just begun. Embrace the challenges, celebrate the successes, and continue to explore the vast and exciting world of JavaScript. The possibilities are endless.

Appendix

This appendix provides supplementary information to enhance your understanding of JavaScript.[1] It includes a list of reserved keywords, common errors and solutions, useful resources, and a glossary of terms.

A.1. JavaScript Reserved Keywords

Reserved keywords are identifiers that cannot be used as variable names, function names, or any other identifier in JavaScript.[2] They have special meanings in the language.

- **Keywords Currently in Use:**
  - break
  - case
  - catch
  - class
  - const

- continue
- debugger
- default
- delete
- do
- else
- export
- extends
- finally
- for
- function
- if
- import
- in
- instanceof
- new
- return
- super
- switch
- this
- throw
- try
- typeof[3]
- var

- void
- while
- with
- yield
- let

- **Keywords Reserved for Future Use:**
  - enum
  - implements
  - interface
  - package
  - private
  - protected
  - public
  - static

A.2. Common JavaScript Errors and Solutions

Understanding common JavaScript errors and their solutions is crucial for effective debugging.

- **SyntaxError:**
  - **Description:** Occurs when JavaScript encounters code that violates the language's syntax rules.[4]
  - **Examples:** Missing semicolons, mismatched brackets, incorrect keywords.[5]
  - **Solution:** Carefully review the error message and the surrounding code. Use a linter to catch syntax errors early.[6]
- **ReferenceError:**
  - **Description:** Occurs when you try to access a variable or function that is not defined.

- **Examples:** Using an undeclared variable, calling a function that doesn't exist.
- **Solution:** Ensure that variables and functions are declared before they are used.[7] Check for typos in variable and function names.

- **TypeError:**
  - **Description:** Occurs when you try to perform an operation on a value of an incorrect type.
  - **Examples:** Calling a method on an undefined object, trying to add a number to a string.
  - **Solution:** Check the types of variables and values before performing operations. Use typeof or instanceof to verify types.

- **RangeError:**
  - **Description:** Occurs when a numeric value is outside the allowed range.

- ○ **Examples:** Passing an invalid value to a function that expects a specific range.[8]
- ○ **Solution:** Validate input values and ensure that they are within the allowed range.[9]
- **URIError:**
  - ○ **Description:** Occurs when you use the encodeURI(), decodeURI(), encodeURIComponent(), or decodeURIComponent() functions with an invalid URI.
  - ○ **Solution:** Ensure that URIs are properly formatted before encoding or decoding them.
- **EvalError:**
  - ○ **Description:** (Deprecated) Occurred when using the eval() function in older JavaScript versions.
  - ○ **Solution:** Avoid using eval() whenever possible.
- **Logical Errors:**

- Description: Occur when your code runs without throwing an error, but it doesn't produce the expected result.
- Examples: Incorrect calculations, wrong conditional statements, infinite loops.
- Solution: Use debugging techniques, such as logging, breakpoints, and code reviews, to identify and fix logical errors.

A.3. Useful JavaScript Resources and Links

- **MDN Web Docs:**
  - https://developer.mozilla.org/en-US/docs/Web/JavaScript
  - A comprehensive resource for web development technologies, including JavaScript.
- **ECMAScript Specification:**

- o https://tc39.es/ecma262/
  - o The official specification for the JavaScript language.
- **freeCodeCamp:**
  - o https://www.freecodecamp.org/
  - o A free, open-source platform that offers coding challenges and projects.
- **Codecademy:**
  - o https://www.codecademy.com/
  - o Offers interactive courses on JavaScript and other programming languages.[11]
- **Udemy:**
  - o https://www.udemy.com/
  - o Provides a wide range of paid and free courses on JavaScript and web development.
- **Stack Overflow:**
  - o https://stackoverflow.com/
  - o A question-and-answer site for programming-related questions.
- **GitHub:**
  - o https://github.com/

- A platform for hosting and collaborating on open-source projects.
-
- **Airbnb JavaScript Style Guide:**
  - https://github.com/airbnb/javascript[12]
  - A widely adopted and comprehensive style guide.
- **ESLint:**
  - https://eslint.org/
  - A pluggable and configurable linter tool for identifying and reporting on patterns found in ECMAScript/JavaScript code.[13]
- **Prettier:**
  - https://prettier.io/
  - An opinionated code formatter.

A.4. Glossary of Terms

- **API (Application Programming Interface):** A set of rules and protocols that allow different software applications to communicate with each other.
- **Asynchronous Programming:** A programming paradigm that allows code to execute non-sequentially, preventing blocking operations.
- **Callback Function:** A function that is passed as an argument to another function and executed when the outer function completes its task.[14]
- **Closure:** A function that remembers its lexical scope, even when it's executed outside of that scope.[15]
- **DOM (Document Object Model):**[16] A programming interface for HTML and XML documents that represents the document as a tree structure.

- **Event Handling:** The process of responding to user actions or other events that occur in the browser.
- **Framework:** A software framework provides a foundation on which software developers can build programs for a specific platform.[17]
- **Hoisting:** A JavaScript mechanism where variable and function declarations are moved to the top[18] of their scope during compilation.[19]
- **JSON (JavaScript Object Notation):** A lightweight data-interchange format that is easy for humans to read and write and easy for machines to parse and generate.[20]
- **Library:** A collection of pre-written code that provides specific functionalities.
- **Module:** A self-contained unit of code that can be imported and exported.[21]
- **npm (Node Package Manager):** A package manager for JavaScript that

allows you to install and manage third-party libraries and modules.[22]

- **Promise:** An object that represents the eventual completion (or failure) of an asynchronous operation and its resulting value.[23]
- **Scope:** The context in which variables and functions are accessible.
- **Syntax:** The set of rules that define the structure of a programming language.
- **Variable:** A named storage location that holds a value.[24]
- **Web API:** An API that is accessible over the web, typically using HTTP.[25]
- **WebAssembly (Wasm):** A binary instruction format for a stack-based virtual machine. Wasm makes it possible to run code written in multiple languages on the web at near-native speed.[26]